Go Clean, Sexy You

A seasonal guide to
detoxing and
staying healthy

Go Clean, Sexy You

A seasonal guide to detoxing and staying healthy

LISA CONSIGLIO RYAN

CERTIFIED HEALTH COACH

SparkPress, a BookSparks Imprint

A Division of SparkPoint Studio, LLC

Published by SparkPress, a BookSparks imprint,
A division of SparkPoint Studio, LLC
Tempe, Arizona, USA, 85281
www.sparkpointstudio.com

All company and/or product names may be trade names, logos,
trademarks, and/or registered trademarks and are the property of their respective owners.

Printed in Canada by Friesens.

Print ISBN: 978-1-940716-91-6
Digital ISBN: 978-1-940716-90-9
Library of Congress Control Number: 2015953520

Cover design by Julie Metz Ltd./metzdesign.com
Interior design by Tabitha Lahr
Cover and author photos: © Suni Danielle Photography
Interior photos: page 109 © Kristin Duvall/Stocksy.com; page 137 © Jeff Wasserman/Stocksy.com; page 187 © Nataša Mandić/Stocksy.com; all others © Suni Danielle Photography

Go Clean, Sexy You is for informational purposes only. Before starting your detox or any dietary changes, consult with your doctor. Results from the detox will vary, as each individual's body is different. Follow your intuition and take the information provided here as suggestions only. The author is not a medical doctor; therefore, this program is not intended as medical advice. Because there is always a risk involved, the author and publisher may not be held responsible for any adverse effects or consequences resulting from the use of any recipes, suggestions, or procedures hereafter.

The author and publisher have no affiliation to organizations, companies and products mentioned in this book. Internet addresses given in this book were accurate at the time it went to press.

For my loves, Kevin, Kate, and Jack.

You bring joy to my life each and every day.

I'm grateful for your support and unconditional love.

Contents

PREFACE 9

INTRODUCTION 13
My Story 13
The Clean Life and the
  80/20 Guideline 18
Relative Balance 19

**CHAPTER 1: GETTING DOWN
WITH DETOX BASICS**
Why pH Balance Is So Important . . . 21
Why Do You Need to
  Detox Anyway? 24
Go Clean, Sexy You Benefits 25
What Should You Expect
  during Detox? 26
Seven Substances to Skip
  during Detox 27
The Dirty Dozen and Clean
  Fifteen Produce 28
Kitchen Gear:
  Six Must-have Tools 30
Detox Staples 33

**CHAPTER 2: HOW TO
USE THIS BOOK**
Guide to Recipes 37
How to Make the Basics 38
Common Detox FAQs 44

**CHAPTER 3: PRECLEANSE AND
DAILY INSTRUCTIONS**
Get Ready! 49
Daily Instructions 52

CHAPTER 4: SPRING DETOX PLAN
Spring Detox Plan 57
Spring Menu Plan 60

Shopping List 62
Recipes 64

**CHAPTER 5: SUMMER DETOX PLAN
(RAW FOOD FOCUS)**
Summer Detox Plan 81
Summer Menu Plan 84
Shopping List 86
Recipes 88

CHAPTER 6: FALL DETOX PLAN
Fall Detox Plan 111
Fall Menu Plan 114
Shopping List 116
Recipes 118

CHAPTER 7: WINTER DETOX PLAN
Winter Detox Plan 133
Winter Menu Plan 138
Shopping List 140
Recipes 142

**CHAPTER 8: "RETURN TO LIFE"
AFTER DETOX**
Next Steps to Keep the
  Glow Going 159
Party in Your Pantry 162
Make Sure Your Clean Pantry
  is Stocked with These Items . . . 164
Bonus Recipes 167

Big Love and Thank You 189
Inspiration and Resources 191
Recommended Reading 193
Recommended Kitchen Gear 194
Testimonials 196
Index 215
About the Author 223

Preface

Well, hello there! Welcome to *Go Clean, Sexy You* . . . and join the revolution.

Yes. Revolution.

What you'll find in this book is not just a bunch of recipes (which are *très* delicious, in fact) but a whole philosophy on how to live your life healthy, happy, and overall free of numbers like calories and grams. Our culture is obsessed with weighing, calorie counting, and other negative ways to treat our bodies. It's time to stop, and I'll show you how.

More and more people are starting to make another choice, a choice to take charge and listen. And I'm hoping you join us.

Who do we listen to? Our bodies.

Our bodies have the answer for healing us.

Our bodies know what we truly need to live optimally healthy lives.

Our bodies know what is best for us, whether it comes to food, our relationships, our work, and our dreams.

Our bodies pump blood without our knowing, breathe for us, keep us alive no matter what. Our bodies love us unconditionally.

When we choose to push and struggle, our bodies fight even harder to keep us in balance.

Our minds can be so powerful, taking charge of our beautiful, wise bodies; analyzing every number on the scale (which we all know, if it's not the number we want, we are in a bad mood for the rest of the day); Googling the latest quick fix; and constantly thinking of ways to fit into that dress size again. Our mind's self-criticism and perfectionism can take over and override the body's messages.

I'm here to support you in taming your mind so you can hear what your lovely body is trying to tell you. You'll be able to overcome the obstacles that leave you feeling exhausted every afternoon, that cause you to repeat unhealthy habits that keep you struggling, and that prevent you from losing those last ten pounds.

As you navigate through the seasons with my whole food–based detox plans, you'll tap into your body's wisdom; form sustainable, healthy habits; and develop a positive, loving, respectful relationship with your body.

There are tons of detox benefits you will be able to reap, but the most important lesson is that you can be free of the chains that keep you stuck and never feeling good enough. This takes time, and I'm here to hold your hand during your wellness journey.

The *Go Clean, Sexy You* revolution is growing bigger each day, with thousands of women (and some cool dudes) listening to their bodies, feeling at ease, and living full, beautiful lives.

When you live the *Go Clean, Sexy You* way, you embody true connection to your body. That's why listening constantly to what your body tells you will be the biggest part of your journey.

A few months ago, a friend and I were joking around, and he said something that cracked me up. But then his comment hit home: *You can't really be sexy unless you are clean.*

Absolutely.

Being clean simply means putting healthy, whole foods into your body; making decisions with integrity; associating with those people who fuel you, not bring you down; and managing stress with activities that bring you back to balance.

When you are clean, you feel light. You have a sparkle in your eyes and glowing skin. Your thoughts are positive and loving, especially toward yourself.

As you walk with confidence because you are clean and light, well, that is true sexiness. Everyone will want what you have. You become a role model for your family, friends, coworkers, and even strangers.

My client Michelle S. from Brooklyn, New York, posted this message, and it's a testament to our mission:

Good morning, sexy beasts!!!

Just dropping a line about how inspiring and amazing each of you are. Every day we make the decision to respect our bodies and lavish them in delicious clean, whole foods. And because we cheerfully tote our water bottles and healthy habits out into the world, OTHER people also reap the benefits!

I was reminded of this when a coworker mentioned that she notices my meals for lunch and she has begun to rethink the way she eats. She even challenged herself to switching from soda to water this week!

There is no telling how many "secret admirers" you have, but even if they don't join the revolution immediately, one thing is for sure—you are planting a seed. Continue being amazing and sharing your love for healthy hearts, minds, and bodies!

xoxo
MS

I invite you to join our *Go Clean, Sexy You* revolution. As you learn how to connect with your body during the year, you'll certainly feel clean and sexy. Plus you'll plant seeds and inspire others to take care of themselves. What a wonderful world it will be when we all nourish ourselves from the inside out, listen to our bodies, and truly live the lives we are meant to live.

Introduction

MY STORY

Food is love.

I didn't always think that way. In fact, food and I didn't quite have a loving relationship while I was growing up and for much of my adult life.

I wish I could say I was always healthy and that I cooked all my meals from scratch. I wish I could tell you that I led a balanced life without much stress or uncertainty. I wish I could report that I wasn't a yo-yo dieter who tried almost every diet on the planet just to lose weight.

Claiming that I have always been happy with my body and how I looked would be a lie.

First of all, I never cooked. Ever.

Would you believe it?

I know what you're thinking: "You're a health coach. I bet you were born with a soup spoon in your hand."

This couldn't be further than the truth. In fact, before I enrolled at the Institute for Integrative Nutrition, I usually went out to eat every night unless my husband, Kevin, cooked our meals. During my single life, I had been known to use my oven as a storage space for winter sweaters. I mean, really, I never used that thing for cooking, so why not! (I remember a scene from *Sex and the City* where Carrie kept her clothes in her stove, too. See, I'm not the only one! But my sweet friends gently reminded me that Carrie is a fictional character.)

Additionally, I wasn't connected to my food. I didn't know where it came from, let alone how to use it to nourish myself.

And I was sick! My health was a mess. I had fibromyalgia, hypothyroidism, candida, rosacea (when your face gets really puffy and red with lots of breakouts), cystitis, and tons of allergies. And I was only thirty years old!

I also hated my body.

My unhealthy relationship with food started a long, long time ago. I remember when it all went down as clear as day.

I was eight years old, dressed in a yellow cowgirl costume, hat upon my wavy brown hair, and tap shoes clickity clacking on the pavement. I was posing for photos before the big dance recital. I was smiling for the photograph. I was happy.

I felt like a superstar, which was uncommon for me because I was usually painfully shy. But that day, I felt on top of the world, ready to dance my heart out.

Then it happened. Someone I adored said, "You better watch it. You're getting chunky. You don't want to get fat, do you?"

Done.

I stopped eating.

At such a young age, I began to learn that to gain approval from others, to be good enough, I needed to be skinny.

The message became clear and became my mantra.

"I'm not good enough."
"I'm not good enough."
"I'm not good enough."

I took this to heart and began counting the items of food I put in my mouth. I even kept a journal and listed what I ate each day.

I only allowed myself five items of food a day, such as one piece of toast, one stick of bubble gum, and so on..I did this until I was in middle school. I beat myself up if I had one too many pizza slices or inhaled a bag of Hershey's Kisses. Of course, I was growing and I was starving; therefore, a trip to McDonald's would inevitably happen. Afterward, I would feel defeated, then resentful of my body, telling her to listen and not eat so much. This went on for years.

Over time, I developed an unhealthy relationship with food and my body. I was never satisfied with how I looked and especially how I felt. I tried every diet to control what I ate and to lose weight. Little did I know I was making things worse. Quick fixes weren't the answer, and I just couldn't shed pounds no matter how hard I tried. This made me anxious and depressed.

All I thought about was food.

"How many calories are in this yogurt?"
"How many fat grams does this piece of cake have?"
"Is eating one slice of pizza going to make me fat?"

I even negotiated exercise when I ate food.

"If I eat those chips, I will run an extra five miles tomorrow."
"I will work out two hours every day this week to burn off all the calories from the weekend."

I tried EVERYTHING to lose weight, including these tricks:
- Atkins Diet
- South Beach Diet (I stayed on this one for almost three years . . . never moved to Phase II—no fruit for years because it was a sugar. Crazy pants!)
- Low-fat and low-carb diets (I can remember my plates being all white with the rice and pasta)
- SlimFast
- Two-hour workouts seven days a week (I was exhausted!)
- Workouts two times a day at the gym (still exhausted!)
- Body for Life program (before my wedding)

- Weight Watchers (I joined after having my daughter, Kate. I actually gained weight—thought I would get my points for the day with cookies instead of a healthy snack)

I would gain a few pounds, lose them, and gain even more back.

After having my babies, things got worse. I constantly exercised. I didn't eat or only pretended to eat in front of my kids. I avoided anything with sugar or carbs, so that meant even fruit never touched my lips.

One day, my little three-year-old Kate said, "Mamma, why aren't you eating with us? Why don't you eat?"

She was watching me.

I didn't want my daughter to see this. I didn't want anyone to feel the pain I knew, especially my own child. I knew I had to get help.

Even though I had my struggles, there was a silver lining.

While this was happening, I realized that I was the go-to girl if anyone had a question about natural health and fitness. As an elementary school teacher for fifteen years, I was also passionate about education. Getting my certification as a health coach allowed me to combine my passions: nutrition and education. I learned how to cook real, whole food; establish family dinners; and resolve my dysfunctional relationship with food once and for all. In fact, I no longer have any of those health issues I mentioned earlier. I don't even think about diets or calories. I feel so free!

I EAT. I eat what makes me feel good. I treat my body with respect. I listen to HER.

I am REAL. Life is easier and full.

Don't get me wrong, these feelings didn't happen overnight. The freedom I feel today took a while to accomplish. Lots of practice, self-love, and patience. Plus tons of support.

Does this struggle resonate with you on some level?

Do you want to learn how to take care of your body without beating her up with negative self-talk?

Do you want to stop spending tons of money on fad diet books and pills?

Do you want to learn how to cook whole, real meals that nourish your body as well as your soul?

Do you just want to feel free and liberated from thinking of food all the time?

Well, I am here to tell you that all this—and more—is possible. I totally get where you are coming from. There are still days when I struggle with managing my company, taking care of the kids, and just leading a busy life, but I remind myself to walk the talk. If I tell a client to put kale in that smoothie, I make sure I do the same.

I now believe FOOD IS LOVE. I truly believe it. The more whole, REAL foods we eat, the more REAL we become. Imagine how we can change the world by transitioning to the clean life together.

What is my mantra these days, you ask?

"I AM enough."
"I AM enough."
"I AM enough."

And so are you.

I can help you reach your health goals without deprivation, quick fixes, or exercising two hours a day. I can help you feel connected to your body so that you intuitively tap into your body's wisdom and develop a way of life that allows you to feel liberated and free . . . the *Go Clean, Sexy You* way!

Get ready to have the best year of your life!

THE CLEAN LIFE AND THE 80/20 GUIDELINE

As a health coach, I practice a holistic approach to nutrition and healthy living. As we work together, you will discover how all the parts of your life affect the health and well-being of your whole self. For example, does stress at your job or in your relationship cause you to overeat? Does lack of sleep or low energy prevent you from exercising or preparing healthy meals for yourself and your family? In our society, we are constantly multitasking, juggling the endless responsibilities of our lives and those around us. Stress is the number one cause of inflammation, so that busy syndrome can be numbing. Inflammation leads to chronic disease, but there's more info about that in the pH section.

From having a career to taking care of our families to making time to be with our partners, who really has the time for maintaining good health and emotional well-being?

Well, the answer is YOU do, and I can help you learn how. As we work together to transition to the "clean life," we will develop a plan of action that consists of adding in real, whole food, plus finding ways to manage stress and maintain a healthy weight.

What is the "clean life," you ask? Here's the definition:

You strive to eat anti-inflammatory whole foods (a lot of plants and greens, gluten-free grains, and organic produce), you use natural ingredients when cooking, and you are eco-conscious. You tend to follow the 80/20 guideline: 80 percent of the time you eat clean, move your body, practice gratitude; you do what makes you feel amazing. The other 20 percent of the time you drink wine with your girlfriends, eat pizza at the birthday party, skip a workout . . . all without guilt. You listen to your body and tap into the body, mind, and spirit connection.

No single diet works for everyone, so *Go Clean, Sexy You* shows how to tap into your body's wisdom, connect with her, and form habits and rituals that nourish your body as well as your mind and soul. I don't count numbers, calories, or fat grams or even use scales, and neither should you. Diets just don't work. Instead, I'll give you the tools you need to figure out what works best for your body without starving, deprivation, or rules.

RELATIVE BALANCE

Another big part of the clean life is relative balance.

We all want balance:

Balance within ourselves. Physically, our bodies strive for a pH level of 7.365 to keep us at optimum health. Not to get into a big science lesson here, but over time, stress and certain foods like caffeine, processed sugar, dairy, gluten, and animal protein can tip our bodies over to the acidic side, which leads to inflammation and then chronic disease. Now this takes a LONG time to happen, but if you don't reset your body, this can happen. Our bodies want balance to ensure we keep living. That is why a clean life is so important. By pumping clean foods like veggies and fruit into our bodies, we can rebalance our blood to a good pH level and become less acidic. Therefore, our organs get a break and don't have to work so hard fighting off inflammation.

Balance with nature. We tend to eat more warm soups and stews in winter and more raw vegetables and cool drinks in summer.

Balance with each other. No one can really say she likes conflict. I don't. I try to avoid it at all costs. We need to feel connected globally to be balanced.

So yeah, losing some belly fat or having glowing skin would be nice—in fact, fabulous—but living the clean life is so much more than that. Finding relative balance is the goal of the *Go Clean, Sexy You* way and the route to leading a healthy and happy life. Keep in mind that we can't be perfect. Let's face it, we are human and can't control everything in our environment. But we can make an effort to control what we are eating and how we deal with stress.

Pay close attention to that relative balance as you ease into the *Go Clean, Sexy You* life. How does your balance shift? What feels good? Not so good?

There are no quick fixes. So come with me, and I'll show you the ins and outs of how to lead a healthy, fulfilled, and clean life.

I'm so grateful you are here with me during this wellness journey!

CHAPTER 1

Getting Down with Detox Basics

WHY PH BALANCE IS SO IMPORTANT

Do you remember learning about pH back in high school? I recall my chemistry teacher handing us pH strips to test different solutions in beakers. Little did I know then that pH value is crucial when it comes to detoxing. In fact, the basis of all the work I do with my clients relies on pH, because our bodies need to operate within a certain pH level to function at optimal health. The relative balance needed for a clean, sexy life is based on pH, too.

So here's a quickie lesson:

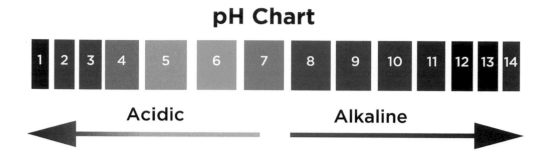

The measure of acidity and alkalinity is referred to pH, which means "power of hydrogen" or "potential of hydrogen." It is measured on a scale ranging from pH 1 (most acidic) to pH 14 (most alkaline).

As I mentioned in the introduction, your body maintains balance and thrives at a 7.365 pH. This balance is vital, especially in the blood. If the body's blood pH drops (becomes too acidic), the likelihood of illness and disease will increase. This takes time, a lot of time, but if you are constantly eating acidic foods (coffee, sugar, fast food), participating in acidic behaviors (stress, worry, negativity), and not getting a body reboot with detox, you will have a hard time losing weight, will feel tired and blah (not to mention stressed out), and will end up very, very sick.

All this happens at the cellular level, so paying attention to your blood's pH can give you tons of insight on what is going on inside your body.

Now it's okay if you fluctuate a bit on the pH scale now and then, because your body does an amazing job gathering minerals such as calcium, iron and magnesium to address the acidity. These minerals are pulled from your teeth, bones and organs to neutralize the acidity.

But if your body is constantly taxed with exposure to toxins and operating at an acidic level, you may be setting yourself up over time not only for colds and flu, candida/yeast issues, and obesity but also osteoporosis, diabetes, heart disease, cancer, and many other chronic illnesses.

Never fear, though: there's a way to keep things in check and avoid illness.

During detox and for 80 percent of your *Go Clean, Sexy You* daily life, you'll eat alkaline or neutral foods and avoid or limit acidic foods.

ALKALINE/NEUTRAL	ACIDIC
Avocados	Alcohol
Beans and lentils	Animal protein
Cold-pressed oils	Artificial sweeteners
Dark leafy greens	Coffee, soda (any: caffeinated or decaffeinated)
Oranges, grapefruits, lemons, limes	Drugs
Quinoa	Heavily processed foods, including soy
Raw nuts and seeds	Processed sugars and substitutes
Seasonal fruits (mainly berries)	Refined grains and wheat (gluten)
Vegetables (including root veggies)	Salted and roasted nuts
Water	Table salt (sea salt or kosher salt are better substitutes)

How do you find out about your body's pH level? Easy.

The most accurate way to test your pH is to use pH strips. You can buy them at any natural food store. Just urinate (test your second "pee" of the day) and violà—you'll have amazing insight to your body's condition.

Detoxing is a wonderful way to reset your cells and give you a pH makeover, especially when the change of the season puts stress on your body. Keep your pH lesson in the back of your mind as you go through your year with detox and see how your gorgeous body thrives with eating alkaline foods as well as leading an alkaline (stress-free) life.

WHY DO YOU NEED TO DETOX ANYWAY?

As humans, we are constantly exposed to toxins beyond our control. And many of us eat and drink substances that are addictive and processed.

Over the past seventy years or more, the Western world has seen a tremendous increase in the use of chemicals in all types of industry, including factory farming. This dependence on chemicals has brought with it a ton of toxins. Our soil has been depleted of nutrients; pesticides corrupt the crops. So most of the fruits and vegetables we get now can't compare to the nice, healthful produce people ate years and years ago.

Plus many supplies we use to clean our homes and cars, even the makeup and body lotions we put on our skin, are toxic. Over time, everyday toxins seep into our skin, our tissues, and our cells and accumulate in our organs, our blood, and especially in our digestive system. We become acidic, and our bodies are in danger of disease.

The main toxins are . . .
- The air you breathe
- The water you drink
- The food you eat
- The medications and cosmetics you use
- The body's own toxins

When your body is overloaded with toxins, your organs in turn work overtime to eliminate pain and inflammation rather than help you look radiant, feel energized, and have optimal health.

During detox, all the main organs (liver, kidneys, skin, lymphatic system, intestines, and lungs) work together to rebuild your system and reduce your toxic load. Therefore, cleansing each season is recommended to keep your body free of chronic illness as well as well as keep you looking and feeling young and sexy.

Detox is beneficial to anyone experiencing:

- Digestive problems
- Excess weight
- Headaches
- Mood swings
- Acne and/or eczema
- Allergies
- Slow metabolism
- Body aches and pains
- Premature aging
- Lack of energy

The results of a detox may include clear, glowing skin, weight loss, better sleep, more energy, bright eyes, and much more. Let's look more closely at them.

GO CLEAN, SEXY YOU BENEFITS

There are TONS of amazing benefits you can receive each time you detox during the year:

- With detox, you can easily lose the extra "fluff" and feel lighter again quickly. Perhaps you need to lose weight in winter because you've been inactive and eaten too many comfort foods. Or you reboot in spring to look amazing in your bathing suit. Overindulging in trips, cookouts, and barbecues may call for a summer detox. In autumn, you detox to get yourself ready for the holidays.
- Our bodies strive for balance with nature, so as each season shifts, our bodies need support through nourishing foods. Soups and stews in the winter, lots of greens in spring, raw foods in summer, and pumpkin and butternut squash in the fall. During the *Go Clean, Sexy You* detox, you'll eat seasonal foods that support your system so that you

enter each time of the year balanced and able to protect yourself against allergies, colds, and flu as well as ease stress due to seasonal changes in weather.

- You connect with the seasons and start to notice the difference between stress eating and real hunger. You will receive insight about your own emotional or mindless eating.

Here are some of the changes I've seen in my own life, as well as in the thousands of women who have detoxed with me:

- Average weight loss of four to ten pounds, so you can fit into your clothes comfortably and not stress about showing some skin with skirts or a bathing suit
- Decreased belly fat and bloating
- Feeling lighter and noticing clothes loosening up
- Tons of energy so you can accomplish a lot in your day (no need to resort to the vending machine or the local Starbucks for the midafternoon pick-me-up)
- Vanished sugar cravings
- Increased libido (oh yes!)
- Best, sound sleep ever (no getting up to use the bathroom, no insomnia, etc.)
- Glowing, clear, dewy skin (my favorite side effect)
- Bright, sparkly eyes (I love this one, too!)

All of these amazing detox perks work to reset your body's metabolism and help you develop lifelong, sound nutritional habits. You'll be a great role model for your family and friends even as you live a long *Go Clean, Sexy You* life!

WHAT SHOULD YOU EXPECT DURING DETOX?

Days 1 to 3: You might want to kill me during these first few days, especially if you currently drink a lot of caffeine and eat a lot of sugar. (Don't worry, though, I will give you instructions on how to wean before the cleanse!) I have to be honest about that reaction. It's different for everyone, of course, but you might feel a headache or be a bit tired. This is completely normal!

Days 4 to 7: As you shift away from foods that are typically hard to digest, allergenic, or addictive, you will notice positive changes in your body, energy levels, and mood. You will be thinking, "Yeah, baby, I got this! Feelin' good!"

Days 6 to 10: Bingo! You are feeling on top of the world. You will have the momentum to continue living clean. You will feel that balance within your body. Also, watch your friends and family, because you might notice that they change, too. They will want what you have!

Note: If you are doing the summer raw cleanse included in this book, you will feel the raw glow in just a few days. With raw food, you are not manipulating the energetic qualities of the food, so you're getting the most nutrients and enzymes possible to light up your tissues and cells more quickly than with foods that have been baked, steamed, or boiled.

SEVEN SUBSTANCES TO SKIP DURING DETOX

There are no ifs, ands, or buts about omitting the following. (I know . . . I'm mean, but it's for your own good, I promise.)

Processed Foods

Foods that come in bags and boxes contain artificial ingredients and additives that make the body work extra hard. Let your body take a break by enjoying real foods in their natural form.

Caffeine

Caffeine, whether it's in the form of coffee or soda, may give you a false energy boost that can cover up bad food choices and lack of sleep. Coffee and soda are highly acidic, which makes them tough on your digestive system, let alone your whole body.

Added Sugar

By this I mean granulated sugar and high fructose corn syrups as well as all those crack sugar substitutes that come in packets. (Yes, I'm being harsh, but I don't tolerate these substances!) These substances are highly processed and have zero nutrients for our bodies. We don't need this type of sugar. Also, research shows that these sugars may be just as addictive as drugs like cocaine. In excess, it leads to weight gain and tons of inflammation.

Dairy

I can go on and on about the disadvantages of dairy, since we just don't need this type of food in our lives. But simply explained, even if you aren't allergic, you could benefit from a dairy break. Dairy can be the root of feeling sluggish, bloated, and congested.

Gluten

If you feel tired, bloated, or moody, you may be gluten intolerant and not even know it. When you stop eating this form of protein found in wheat, rye, and barley, you might notice a big improvement in your energy—and that muffin top might disappear.

Soy

Since soy has become an allergen and highly controversial when it comes to hormones and the reproductive system, we will omit this food for detox. Unfortunately in North America, soy is now highly processed (think frozen veggie burgers and hotdogs), which means we're mostly not getting the healthy, fermented soy which is found in the East.

Alcohol

Not only can booze mess with your metabolism and cause you to gain weight from all its empty calories, alcohol can interfere with sleep and also make your beautiful liver work overtime.

All recipes and plans in this book are plant-based. Therefore in addition to avoiding the above substances, we will be omitting animal protein.

THE DIRTY DOZEN AND CLEAN FIFTEEN PRODUCE

During detox, chose your produce wisely. Refer to the Shopper's Guide to Pesticides in Produce to learn more about the Dirty Dozen and the Clean Fifteen. Visit the Environmental Working Group at www.ewg.org to download your free list of the least and most pesticide-laden produce. You can even get a free app for your phone to keep up to date with the rankings. Shop smarter and make informed choices about the produce you buy.

When in doubt, go for organic. It doesn't make sense to detox and then add toxins back into the body.

Dirty Dozen

The Dirty Dozen Plus consists of the produce grown with the most pesticides, ranked from bad to terrible. The rankings change slightly from year to year. It's updated regularly on ewg.org, so check the list often. Whenever produce appears on the Dirty Dozen list, aim to buy the organic instead of the conventional kind.

1. Apples
2. Peaches
3. Nectarines
4. Strawberries
5. Grapes
6. Celery
7. Spinach
8. Bell Peppers
9. Cucumbers
10. Cherry Tomatoes
11. Snap peas
12. Potatoes

+

13. Hot Peppers
14. Kale/Collard Greens

Clean Fifteen

The foods on the Clean Fifteen list are grown with the least amount of pesticides, ranked from best to okay on ewg.org. (This list can also change from year to year.) If you are on a budget, it's okay to buy the conventionally grown (nonorganic) forms of this produce:

1. Avocados
2. Sweet Corn
3. Pineapple
4. Cabbage
5. Sweet peas (frozen)
6. Onions
7. Asparagus
8. Mangos
9. Papayas
10. Kiwifruit
11. Eggplant
12. Grapefruit
13. Cantaloupe
14. Cauliflower
15. Sweet potatoes

KITCHEN GEAR: SIX MUST-HAVE TOOLS

Do you like to collect all kinds of gadgets? Is your countertop full of things you never ever use? Like ever?

My hand is raised up high. I recently did a massive decluttering job to weed out unwanted gear. I felt amazing when I did that! I no longer feel stressed out when I enter the kitchen. I feel relieved and have space to think about what I want to cook (or create . . . I think cooking is such an art!).

When your kitchen is cluttered, your mind gets all jumbled up and it's hard to make healthy decisions because you are stressed about the mess. At that point, it seems easier to just pick up takeout and ignore all those Pampered Chef party items you just had to buy and which are now littering your counter.

I've narrowed down kitchen gear to the six absolute basic tools you need for your detoxes. The following handy-dandy tool guide sets up your kitchen with the basics. You can add that dehydrator, mandoline, or garlic press (which almost made it on the top six list) in the future. Let's stick to the most important items for a clean kitchen.

So before you start your detox, make sure your kitchen is stocked with the following gear so you can get to *Go Clean, Sexy You* eating!

1. Knife

Before purchasing a knife, hold it in your hand because your personal comfort is the most important factor to consider. Try out many styles and brands before you commit.

I recommend purchasing one knife you will use often rather than a whole set as it can be quite expensive. Build your own set over time, selecting knives that will fit your lifestyle.

Start out with a 8-10 inch chef knife. There are a few styles to choose from. Japanese-style brands such as the NHS are light and tend to have thin blades while German-style brands are heavier with thicker blades. My favorite is the ceramic knife. It is light, super sharp and fits well with my wrist. Go to your local Sur la Table or Bed Bath and Beyond to test-drive a few different types before you purchase.

After you choose your chef knife, work your way to the paring knife and a knife with a serrated-edge (great for cutting sushi, gluten-free breads, etc…). Check out www.justknives101 .com for info on all types of knives and how to care for them.

Tip: Amazon Prime anyone? If you find a knife you want, check out Amazon to see if it offers a discount and free shipping on the brand you've selected. Compare prices and get the best deal.

2. Bamboo Cutting Board

Cutting boards made of bamboo are better for the environment because bamboo is a renewal resource. Let's keep it green!

A good-size board can be heavy so choose a size that will fit on your countertop. Choose an expandable board that fits over your sink if you are tight on space.

There are great selections available in stores and online from www.cooking.com and Bed Bath and Beyond.

Note: Make sure to clean the cutting board frequently with hot, soapy water to avoid bacteria build up.

3. Storage Containers

The *Go Clean, Sexy You* lifestyle features plenty of gluten-free grains, nuts, seeds and legumes so it's a good idea to always have storage containers with airtight lids on hand. In order to keep food fresh longer, glass is the best choice over plastic.

You can pick up a nice four-piece set, like the Libbey glass canisters with stainless steel lids at Bed Bath and Beyond. Place these pretty canisters on the countertop for quick access while cooking.

My favorite is Snapware containers. When my box of Snapware Glasslock Set arrived from Amazon, I almost fainted with joy.

Check out www.containerstore.com and www.worldkitchen.com for Snapware and Pyrex (another great brand of glass containers packages). These sites have everything for the container lover.

Oh, and I use mason jars to store not only the beans and grains, but juices, smoothies, and even salads for the week (check out page 40 for salad jar instructions). You can grab a 12 pack at Target, Amazon, just about anywhere that sells canning supplies.

4. Quality Set of Pots and Pans

Since microwaving changes the nutrients of food and can be harmful to your health, I recommend cooking with pots and pans as much as possible. Don't stress, though. Do what you can but start thinking of limiting your time with the microwave.

That said; let's talk about pots and pans.

Try starting with these basic sizes to get you on your way to preparing healthy meals:

- 3-quart sauté pan
- 2–4 quart saucepan
- 6–8 quart stockpot

What kind of pots and pans to buy? I recommend purchasing the highest quality you can afford. Cookware is an investment. Most with porcelain-enamel coating are safe, look beautiful and are easy to clean. They are great for slow-cooking soups and stews, too. The two top brands are Le Creuset and Chantal. Check them out at www.lecreuset.com and www.chantal.com.

Cast iron cookware is another type I recommend. I just love my cast iron skillet. I love making the GF Banana Oat Muffins (see page 182) in my skillet. Yum! You can make so many delicious meals (even pancakes, gluten-free of course) with your case iron cookware, even sautéing veggies. You can find good quality cast iron cookware at Bed Bath and Beyond.

I also cook with stainless steel pots and pans. These can be less expensive than the cast iron and porcelain-enamel but will do the trick. The brands I recommend are All-Clad (www.allclad.com) and Calphalon (www.caphalon.com).

Note: Stay away from Teflon. Teflon is toxic to humans and the environment, and while you might think "non-stick" is a better option, stick to the above materials (use low to medium heat temperatures) in order to play it safe.

5. Salad Spinner

On the *Go Clean, Sexy You* plan, we eat a lot of greens, and we don't want them turning brown in a few days. (See my website for tips on how to Keep Your Greens Fresh.)

A salad spinner allows you to wash your greens and dry them at the same time. Also, using a salad spinner is more environmentally friendly. You can waste a lot of paper towels trying to blot the leaves after washing!

My favorite is the OXO Good Grips Salad Spinner. After you are done spinning away, store your freshly washed greens and herbs in the basket by covering them with a damp paper towel and storing in the refrigerator. The outer part of the spinner can be used as a serving bowl.

6. Blender

A blender has so many uses: blend, chop, liquefy, purée, emulsify, and grind. Blenders make a silkier puréed soup than a food processor because their blades whirl at a much higher speed. Having a blender opens up so many possibilities: smoothies, soups, stews, nut butters, dips, and desserts.

I recommend purchasing a high-powered blender such as the Vitamix or Blendec. Both machines are efficient and fast when it comes to preparation.

I'm in love with my Vitamix, and it's the last blender I will ever buy. If you want a less expensive brand, try Breville and KitchenAid. Blenders range in price from $50 to $700, so do your research and pick one that works best for you.

BONUS: Rice Cooker

If you find yourself cooking gluten-free grains often, a rice cooker will be super useful. Rice cookers are available in stovetop or electrical models, and they prepare grains quickly as well as perfectly each time. I also cook my quinoa and beans in this appliance.

Most cookers are easy to use. Just add the grains and water then turn on. Also, almost all models have an automatic "keep warm" function to keep the grains heated until you're ready to serve. My Cuisinart CRC400 Rice Cooker and Steamer does that, and I never burn grains anymore! Sweet!

DETOX STAPLES

Every *Go Clean, Sexy You* kitchen needs the following ingredients:

Fresh Produce

Kale, spinach, cucumbers, leeks, strawberries . . . the list goes on and on. You will be eating all the real, whole goodness from the earth during your detox.

Gluten-Free Grains and Pseudograins

Eating clean reduces your exposure to gluten. For detox, in fact, gluten is eliminated. The primary grain you will find on the *Go Clean, Sexy You* menu is quinoa (technically a pseudograin, or a food that resembles grain but is not technically a grain). Quinoa is a gluten-free wonder food because it provides a complete protein.

You will also see gluten-free rolled oats on the menu. Oats are naturally gluten-free but can become contaminated by being processed in plants that also process wheat, rye, or barley. Look for certified gluten-free oats to be certain.

Another gluten-free grain you will find is millet. Millet is wonderful for a side dish or breakfast.

Most grains can be cooked at a ratio of one cup grain to two cups water, and all grains, except millet, benefit from presoaking and rinsing before cooking. You can soak your grains for one to twenty-four hours. Why soak? Presoaking grains washes away much of the phytic acid that affects mineral absorption, allows them to cook faster, and makes them easier to digest. If you don't have time to soak, no worries. Just add some sea salt to the grains and cook on.

I use my rice cooker to prepare quinoa and other gluten-free grains. But if you want to go old school, here's how to cook grains:

Place grains and water in pot and bring to boil. Reduce heat to a simmer, cover, and cook until all liquid is absorbed. Remove from heat and serve.

Note: Seaweed is an amazing superfood and can be incorporated into your diet after detox, but to keep ingredients as simple as possible, you won't need it for the *Go Clean, Sexy You* recipes. That said, if you want to use kombu during the grain presoaking process, please do. This type of seaweed helps neutralize the acid-forming property of the grains and assists with digestion.

Nondairy Milk

Typically, I use coconut milk and almond milk for detox recipes. These are the easiest to come by and taste great.

Always look for plain, unsweetened milks. You can have fun by making your own milks too (see p. 108).

Legumes and Lentils

Lentils, chickpeas, white beans, black beans, adzuki . . . all are packed with protein and fiber. A must for our detox recipes!

But if you want to avoid feeling bloated or having gas, you need to soak your beans before cooking. Place beans in pot, cover with water, and soak for several hours—overnight, if time permits. When ready to cook, drain water and rinse beans. If you want to do a quick soak, rinse beans well, place in pot, and cover with water. Bring to boil. Remove from heat, cover, and let sit for one hour. Drain water and rinse beans.

Preparing soaked beans is easy. Fill pot (I use my rice cooker!) with six cups water and bring to boil. Add three cups of beans. Skim off and discard the foam at top of pot. Reduce heat, cover, and simmer until beans are tender. Remove from heat, drain liquid, and serve.

In the *Go Clean, Sexy You* recipes, I use canned beans to save time. Make sure you buy a brand that stores the beans in BPA-free cans.

Note: Cook beans immediately after soaking to avoid growth of bacteria.

Seeds and Nuts

We'll be eating up almonds, walnuts, pine nuts, pecans, pumpkin seeds, sesame seeds, hemp seeds, chia seeds, and more during our detox. Raw almond butter will be used for our smoothies.

Oils

I mainly stick to cold or expeller-pressed, unrefined oils for the recipes. The primary oils are extra virgin olive oil and virgin coconut oil.

Apple Cider Vinegar and Fermented Foods

Apple cider vinegar: ahhhh, something you will learn to love (hopefully!). Its healing properties are amazing.

You'll see that nutritional yeast appears during your summer detox. This yeast has a cheesy flavor and tastes great sprinkled on salads.

Cooking Wines

Red wine vinegar and balsamic vinegar make appearances during detox. These cooking wines add flavor to food as well as keep blood sugar levels in check.

Herbs and Spices

To jazz up any meal, incorporating fresh herbs such as mint, parsley, and basil and spices such as cumin, cinnamon, and ginger will make your taste buds sing.

CHAPTER 2

How to Use This Book

Go Clean, Sexy You will help you discover new things about your body. How glorious! Before you start, however, here's what you need to know about *Go Clean, Sexy You:*

GUIDE TO RECIPES

I'm Italian and that means I cook by throwing a little of this, a little of that together to make a delicious meal. I rely heavily on my instincts and use spices and herbs to jazz up salads, soups and even snacks. I invite you to do the same. I seldom measure and count (except for testing the *Go Clean Sexy You* recipes) so choose to follow along with exact amounts listed in recipes or experiment. Most recipes make 1-2 servings but double ingredients to have extra for left-overs or to share with a loved one.

Add, omit, and substitute as you wish. Make these recipes your own. That way you will learn how to adjust ingredients according to what your body needs the most. Check in with your body and eat until you are just about 80 percent full.

You can follow the menu plan and recipes to a T or mix and match each day. When I say "handful" in regards to nuts and seeds, I mean 1-2 ounces (10 nuts equal 1 serving). Don't weigh the food, but use your hands as a guiding measuring tool. During your cleanses, we want to get away from numbers and counting and begin to listen to our bodies.

Also, you will notice that I repeat Days 1-5 detox meals for Winter, Spring and Fall for Days 6-10. This is done for three reasons:

1. For proper digestion and elimination.
2. To keep expenses low at the grocery store, especially if you are new to clean eating and have a budget.
3. So you aren't making tons of different meals, with different ingredients for the whole 10 days (excluding Summer detox). Keeping things easy peasy is the name of the game.

You are welcome to use the Bonus recipes for substitutes if needed. Just remember to adjust your shopping list before you head to the store.

HOW TO MAKE THE BASICS

Throughout *Go Clean, Sexy You,* you'll need a few basic cooking methods to keep things simple.

How to Cook Gluten-Free Grains

You can make your grains ahead of time according to package directions or use this formula:

1 cup gluten-free grain
2 cups water

Directions: Drain and rinse before cooking. Combine grain with water in rice cooker or pot. Bring to a boil, then simmer uncovered until water is absorbed. Makes 2 cups of gluten-free grain.

Note: An economical solution to buying organic grains is getting them from the bulk bins at your local grocery store. Use the approximate ounce units listed in the recipes to help you select the right amount. If your store doesn't have bulk bins, you can purchase prepackaged grains. There are a variety of brands and ounce sizes to choose from, but I suggest:

Bob's Red Mill Gluten-Free Rolled Oats (32 ounces)
Arrowhead Mills Millet (28 ounces)
Quinoa (14 ounces)

These bags contain more than you will need for each detox, but you can store them in airtight glass containers for future meals.

How to Cook Legumes

In the *Go Clean, Sexy You* recipes, you will use canned beans to save time. Make sure to buy a brand that stores the beans in BPA cans such as Eden Foods.

Always rinse before cooking to avoid bloating and gas.

If you are using dried beans, make sure to add these to your shopping list and use this formula for cooking:

3 cups beans or lentils
6 cups water

Directions: Place beans in bowl and cover with water. Soak overnight. When ready to cook, fill rice cooker or pot with water. Bring to boil. Add legumes. Skim off and discard the foam at the top. Remove from heat, cover and let sit for one hour. Drain water and rinse beans. I recommend making a big batch of legumes so you can have them on hand for the week.

Bonus: Use a pressure-cooker to shorten cooking time and lock in nutrients.

How to Make Salad Jars

Tend to forget to bring your lunches to work? I have a nifty trick for you.

Make a bunch of salad jars during your detox so you can just grab and go. Plus your coworkers will envy you!

What you will need:

A few 32 oz. mason canning jars. Use the wide mouth ones so it's easier to get items in the jar. And all kinds of yummy ingredients for your salad creations.

One thing to remember about salad in a jar is that your dressing goes on the bottom and you should only use things that do well "marinating" in dressing (like hearty veggies, beans, etc.) for the next layer as it's going to be touching the dressing. The rest is pretty easy, but here's a quick guide on how I made my salads in a jar.

1. Start by putting dressing into the bottom of the jar.
2. Add items that will respond well to marinating in the dressing (ex. cucumbers).
3. Add your remaining veggies, legumes, and greens.
    * red bell pepper
    * avocado sprinkled with lemon juice to prevent browning
    * chickpeas
    * spring mix (lots of this—you can really pack it in)
4. Add remaining ingredients.
    * quinoa
    * nuts

A few more tips:

* The quart sized jars make one big, meal sized salad. You could probably split it between two people if it were being served as a side salad.
* My recipes are just guidelines. Use whatever dressing, veggies, protein, and toppings you like. Have fun experimenting!
* Leave a little room at the top of the jar so that you can shake it up right before serving. It helps make sure all parts of the salad have some dressing.
* You can totally eat the salad out of the jar, but they are a little deep for forks so I like pouring the salad into a dish.

How to Make Smoothies

Enjoy your smoothies just after blending. They are most fresh that way. However, if you can't, store them in mason jars. You can keep most smoothies in the fridge for up to 2 days.

For a frostier smoothie, use a frozen bananas, berries, etc... It's important to peel bananas before you freeze (probably makes sense but I've been known to leave the peel on!). I keep a bunch of already peeled bananas in an airtight glass container in the freezer. I do this with all types of fruit, too. If I have some fresh fruit that is ready to go bad, I toss it in the freezer to save for smoothies. You can also get store bought organic frozen fruit (just make sure there is only fruit in the bags; check ingredients!).

If you want a thinner smoothie, just add more water. If you want a frostier taste, add ice cubes to your smoothies.

For smoothie recipes, you can substitute water for any milk. Most recipes make 18 ounces, 1 serving.

Check out www.wholehealthdesigns.com for smoothie info regarding how to make the ultimate smoothie as well as smoothie jars (same concept as salad jars but with smoothie ingredients).

How to Make Juices

Juicing is different than blending. With juicing you are bypassing the digestive system so your organs get a break. Juicing speeds up detoxification process and feeds your cells liquid nutrition instantly.

If you don't have a juicer or want to invest in one, you can use a blender. Add ½ to 1 cup of water to the ingredients in your juices. You can blend until smooth in your high-powered blender. Drink as a smoothie or eat it as veggie soup. The amounts listed in juice recipes are for juicing, so if you will be blending as a smoothie, cut ingredient quantities in half.

Run all of your ingredients through the juicer, and then drink up. You can store juice in the fridge for a few days, but know that it will separate and lose some of its nutritional power as each day goes by. You may also need to stir or shake it since it will probably separate, but don't let this discourage you. Making juice ahead of time so you have it for the next day is better than not getting in your juice at all.

Note: For juices, experiment with ingredients to fit your taste buds and the serving amount. Vegetable sizes vary, so throw in an extra cucumber or more spinach if you desire.

I'm a juicing fanatic so I have tons of extra information on my website, www.wholehealth designs.com.

Consult your doctor before following any plan regarding food, especially if you are on medication. Find out what is best for you. All the menu plans and recipes in this book incorporate real, whole foods and eliminate allergens like gluten and dairy. But make sure to get the okay from your doctor before you start. If you are pregnant and nursing, you can use recipes here and there for some *Go Clean, Sexy You* fun, but because your body is working hard growing and/or feeding a baby as well as yourself, wait until you are finished breast-feeding to go full-on with detox. Also, toxins can enter your baby's bloodstream, so hold off on the detox until after your child is born.

The detox programs are ten days in duration (except for the summer detox). Why ten days?

If you are consistent with following the menu and recipes, you can see results within seven days. With a ten-day detox, you'll be able to carry the glow even further and start establishing habits to take with you after detox.

Also, we on-the-go women need a plan that is practical as well as effective. Sometimes twenty-one days of detoxing isn't feasible, but ten days is just right.

The summer detox is raw, meaning no food is cooked over 118°F. The summer detox is seven days instead of ten because we aren't changing the energetic qualities of the food with baking and boiling. Think of it as "uncooking." When you eat raw, you reap the rewards more quickly, so seven days works best.

All detoxes correspond to the seasons. As I mentioned in the introduction, we strive for balance in nature. Isn't it amazing how nature knows exactly what we need and when to deliver it?

We crave warm soups and stews in winter. In spring, everything on our plate is green and light. In summer, we want to cool off with smoothies and juices. And in fall, we want pumpkins, butternut squash, and all kinds of foods that contain beta-carotene to prepare our bodies for the cold and flu season coming in winter. The cycle flows so easily, and as humans, we thrive on this balance.

When you detox, it's best to select fresh seasonal foods. This approach is cheaper and the most nourishing for your body.

Everything is planned for you. In *Go Clean, Sexy You,* I take the decision making out of the equation. That way, you don't get stuck on the details of what to buy, how to make the meals, and devising a shopping list. I spell out every detail: every ounce, every thing you need to keep motivated and on track. I tell you what to eat for breakfast, midmorning snack, lunch, midafternoon snack, and dinner. I even tell you how many apples to buy!

Some might call this approach anal (in fact, my friends tell me I have those tendencies!), but it's so necessary for your success. There's no thinking on your part. Nada. You get to concentrate on eating yummy food and taking care of yourself instead of racking your brain over what greens to buy or how many tablespoons of olive oil to use. Most detox programs don't offer this level of detail, because it's a lot of work to pull the lists together for you. But for me, I LOVE to do the work for you because I know from my own experience, and from the thousands of people who have detoxed with me, that having a detailed plan eliminates the struggle and the feelings of being overwhelmed.

Use this book as a guide, not a rulebook. I'm reminded time and time again during a cleanse that life inevitably happens, meaning sometimes we get thrown off course. But that's okay, it really is.

Acceptance of these bumps along the road will free you from the pain of forcing or always analyzing your food choices or exercise habits. It's awesome to have the detox tools in our healthy life toolbox, but remember that these detoxes are only a guideline. Take the backseat and *let your body drive.* I know acceptance is extremely hard to achieve, but I've heard tons and tons of stories, including my own, where once you just let go, the pounds fall off or you are running a 5K or you're sleeping at night. The thing we focus on expands, so if it's a negative thought, it will get bigger. Focusing on how we *want* to feel (what does that look and feel like?) is a better bet. When we really take the time to feel in our body, there's no room for forcing or making rules.

This quote always sets me straight when my mind goes down the inner-critic rabbit hole:

> *The opposite of feeling is forcing. When we force, we cannot feel. When we feel, we cannot force.*
> —Aadil Palkhivala

So as you move through your year with detox, test the waters and form some habits that allow you to feel, not force.

This is the nitty-gritty part of detox, and it's magical. I'm excited to share this experience with you.

COMMON DETOX FAQS

So you got some questions? I got answers, my friend. Detox can be an amazing experience, but knowing the ins and outs of the process is beneficial to a successful cleanse. The following questions were compiled during my work with thousands of clients. You might be asking yourself some of these questions as you embark on this *Go Clean, Sexy You* clean-living adventure. Refer to this section before you start your detox—and during—if concerns come up.

Q: I feel nauseous, bloated, etc. . . Am I doing something wrong?

A: You are not doing anything wrong at all. This is just your body's way of getting rid of the yuck (toxins). Usually by the third or fourth day, things get better. It all depends on your body. Try to drink half your body weight in ounces (water, of course!). Are you getting seven to eight hours of sleep? Limiting stress? Eating every three hours? Look at the whole picture. I promise that things get better.

Note: If you are bloated, chew your food thoroughly, take a probiotic supplement or place a hot water bottle on your tummy to relieve any pain.

Q: Do I have to follow the detox menu and plan? Do I need to stick to the list?

A: You can either follow the detox plan to a T or use it as a guide. You can substitute a dinner for a lunch, or vice versa. You can mix and match the meals, if you want. If you make two servings of a meal, you can freeze the extra or eat it for lunch the next day. This is all about saving time, so you are welcome to do that. Since the detox is for only ten days, you do need to stick to your shopping list, however. Just refer to the foods on the list. Do not add any extras like natural/artificial sugars, processed oils, and so on.

Q: I see juice on the menu. Do I need a juicer for this detox?

A: That depends. You want this to be as simple as possible, so think about your lifestyle. If this is your first time making juice or even being exposed to juicing, I wouldn't buy one. Either use your blender to see if you like the consistency or go to a juice bar. They will make your creations for you. If you have a juicer, good deal. Use your juicer as you see fit.

Q: Where do I get the foods on the shopping list?

A: You can find most of the foods at any grocery store. Check the organic section, especially for the produce. Natural food stores like Whole Foods Market will have most of what you are looking for, too. Ask someone if you need to find a product. Don't spend a lot of time looking for an item. Just ask for help.

Note: You can even grab items online for easy convenience. Seach Amazon or Thrive Market for organic, natural products.

Q: I have a baby shower (birthday dinner, family brunch, etc,) scheduled. What should I do?

A: Make sure you've planned ahead for your week. If you know you are going to be out for a social event, either bring your yummy detox meals or order a dark leafy green salad with tons of fresh veggies. If you need a little somethin' on your salad, try extra virgin olive oil and vinegar. Add lemon juice, too. Remember to be gentle with yourself. If you have a slip at a social event, get back on the horse right after.

Q: I'm tired of water. What else can I drink? Can I drink green tea?

A: You can jazz up your water by adding lemon, lime, cucumbers, or even frozen fruit. You can try adding an herbal tea bag to a pitcher of water in the fridge. You can drink any herbal tea. Green tea has caffeine, so stick to caffeine-free teas.

Q: I can't find Swiss chard (or kale or other greens). What can I use instead?

A: Sometimes grocery stores might not carry certain greens. No worries. Just substitute any dark leafy green in the recipe. Most will work. Try spinach, kale, collards, Swiss chard, dandelion greens . . . the list goes on.

Q: What kitchen items do I need for the cleanse?

A: Begin with a blender, a cutting board, and a good knife. Refer to "Kitchen Gear: Six Must-have Tools" in Chapter 1 for details of what you'll need and why. As for a juicer, don't invest unless you plan on juicing on a regular basis.

Q: I work out a lot. Can I do this detox?

A: Absolutely. The detox plans in this book are geared toward active people. You can cleanse and rid your body of toxins without putting your life on hold. Make sure to eat all your meals and snacks. If you need extra protein or fat, go for it. Listen to your body. Also, if you feel as if you need to back off on exercise intensity, do so.

Q: Do I need to stick by a toilet while on the detox?

A: No. However, you might be constipated or go to the bathroom a little more often than usual. This is natural as your body expels toxins, especially at the beginning of the cleanse. You are eating normal food. In fact, you're eating real, whole food. Therefore, you body will begin to balance itself out and become regular. See your doctor if you have blood in your stools, though, as this is not part of detox.

Q: How do I wean off the caffeine and sugar so my first detox days aren't miserable?

A: At least a week before your cleanse, start the weaning process. If you drink caffeine, try two cups of coffee a day instead of four. Begin to limit so that the day before your cleanse, you are either not drinking coffee or are limited to one cup (half decaf and half caf). Same goes for sugar. Begin to limit, step by step. Also switch out any artificial sugar with natural sugar such as stevia. By the time day 1 rolls around, you shouldn't be using added sugar or processed foods (since they are full of sugar!) in your diet. Do your best. These two substances are very addictive. Take it easy, be gentle on yourself, and limit as much as you can before your first day of detox.

Q: How many calories are in this detox?

A: The estimated caloric intake ranges from 1,200 to 1,500 a day. This is approximate and will depend on servings of meals and portions for each meal plan.

Q: What if I have a food allergy?

A: Most allergens such as dairy, gluten, soy are eliminated during detox. If you have other allergies, you can always omit the ingredients that aggravate your condition.

Q: How should I prepare?

A: Let's be honest. Planning = Success. The best advice is first to decide on your start date. Go shopping at least one to two days before your detox day, cut and chop any veggies and bag them for snacks the night before, and make a few meals ahead of time. That way you can freeze or refrigerate the meals and save them for nights you get home late or when an emergency comes up.

Q: How often can I do a detox?

A: It is suggested to do a food-based cleanse once during each season. The detox plans in this book are geared toward seasonal foods that nourish specific organs. Also, as humans we strive for balance with the seasons, so it's safe to cleanse four times a year.

CHAPTER 3

Precleanse and Daily Instructions

GET READY!

All right, here we go! Don't forget to plan (Planning = Success) and to wean yourself off those seven substances I told you about in Chapter 1 (you know, caffeine, sugar, processed food . . .). If you don't, your first few detox days can be—well, how do I say this?—difficult!

To avoid shocking your body and to ease smoothly into detox, here's your action plan for precleansing.

1. Set a goal or intention. Before you begin your detox, write down one to three goals or intentions you hope to achieve during your detox. Why are you detoxing at a particular time of year? What do you hope to achieve? Write, draw, sketch your goals on paper, make it real, and then post them on the refrigerator, on the bathroom mirror, or in your office so you can reference them often and visualize your success. Referring to your list will keep your eyes on the prize and motivate you to keep going when your enthusiasm occasionally dips.

2. Prepare your loved ones. Your family, friends, even coworkers (especially those you eat meals with) should know how important the detox is to you. Ask for their support. Tell them that you are doing something special for yourself. Stress how crucial your detox is for you so they can support you during the process. It's pretty tough to detox when your partner brings pizza into the house, so make sure everyone knows your plan before you start. Who knows? They might want to join you. I have seen this happen very often, so don't be surprised!

3. Invite a friend to join the fun. Even the most motivated person can derail without accountability. Doing the detox with a partner means you can encourage and cheer each other on. You can trade meals, chat daily about your progress, text or call if you need to have a cup of coffee, and celebrate your wins. It's nice to have someone to commiserate with when you miss that chocolate! Accountability is huge and one of the main reasons for the success of my group programs, so grab a partner and get down with detox together.

4. Start weaning off the seven substances in this order:
- Caffeine
- Sugar
- Processed foods
- Alcohol (if you drink it)
- Dairy
- Gluten
- Soy

Try to wean at least seven days before your detox start date.

Start by cutting caffeine and sugar. For caffeine, limit your use. For example, if you drink three Diet Cokes a day, aim for only one and replace the other two with water or an herbal tea. If you drink four cups of coffee, cut back to two and then switch to half caf/half decaf. For sugar, limit processed foods as much as possible, because artificial and added sugars hide in boxed and bagged products. Also, try using natural sweeteners like stevia or raw honey until your detox begins.

Next, limit any dairy, gluten, alcohol, and soy during the precleansing process. That way you can ease into your detox without shocking your system.

5. Clean out your fridge. Get rid of old produce, leftover meals, and any foods that don't fit into the detox plan. Make room for all the gorgeous veggies, fruits, and greens. I promise when you open up the refrigerator door, you will see beauty!

6. Check your detox shopping list and look in your pantry for items you already have on hand. Make sure you have these basics:

- Filtered water
- Fresh lemons (for morning water especially)
- Extra virgin olive oil
- Raw apple cider vinegar (I use this daily . . . fights any illness, I swear!)
- Sea salt—preferably celtic
- Organic pepper
- An assortment of fresh herbs
- Spices (to jazz up any grain or veggie)

7. Get yourself a detox prezzie. Invest in something that will make your detox more comfortable and fun. I bought a pretty bowl for my salads and a gorgeous crystal-looking glass for my juices. What about a cool travel lunch bag or cooler to tote around all your detox goodies? Fun placemats to use for your meals? How can you feel special during your experience?

Finally, we move to the most important step. Are you ready?

8. Use this special time to take care of *you*. Tell your family and friends that you are taking time for yourself so that they know to either help out with meals or give you some alone time at night. Limit stress as much as possible. Also, your food is so connected to your thoughts. Cherish each bite and take time to breathe and be still. This is a time of connection: to your body, mind, and spirit.

DAILY INSTRUCTIONS

Please follow these guidelines during your detox. I promise you will feel amazing if you do! Who knows, you might develop a few new cool habits along the way.

1. Drink tons of water. Drink a glass of warm water first thing in the morning with the juice from half a lemon squeezed in it. This process breaks down mucus in the body, alkalizes your tissues and jump-starts your metabolism. And drink lots of water throughout the day. A lot! Drinking water helps you feel satisfied, flushes your system, and keeps you hydrated. A lot of times when you have that hunger feeling, you are simply dehydrated. So sip, sip, sip during your detox to avoid headaches or feeling nauseous and tired. Aim for half your body weight in ounces each day (take your weight and divide by two, if you are a numbers girl). Remember, sodas, coffee, caffeinated teas are all prohibited.

2. Take one tablespoon of apple cider vinegar. Add this unfiltered, raw vinegar to a glass of water and gulp it down. Even though it sounds acidic, it is super alkalizing in your body so make sure to start this amazing healthy habit. I recommend Bragg's which can be found in any grocery store. Apple cider vinegar can kick any cold and help with congestion. Here are other benefits: removes body toxins, is rich in enzymes and potassium, boosts immune system, promotes digestion, and gives you a glow (yeah, baby!).

3. Space out your meals. Eating every two to three hours rather than nonstop noshing will keep your metabolism boosted and level, and this practice will allow you to identify real hunger. Since you will be eating like this during your detox, get in the habit before you start. You'll feel a world of difference!

4. Do ten minutes of breathing exercises followed by ten minutes of stretching. This can be reduced to five minutes each if you're strapped for time. The main focus is to be still and quiet. You can do this anytime: morning, night, whenever you have some quiet. Here's a quick breathing exercise:

BREATHE IN/BREATHE OUT EXERCISE
- Place your hands on your knees.
- Close your eyes and take ten deep, cleansing breaths.

- When you inhale, count to six, then exhale to a count of six. These breaths should be slow and steady, filling your lungs. During the inhalation, breathe in health; on exhalation, breathe out waste.
- When you have completed the breaths, give thanks. You can simply say "thanks" or be more specific with your intention for the day. For example, "I am thankful for this journey to wellness," or "I am thankful that I am alive and well" or "Today I will be strong and positive."

5. Before showering, gently dry brush the skin. The best time to dry brush is in the morning but if that doesn't work for you, do it anytime before you shower. You can purchase your body brush at any beauty supply store. The entire dry brushing process takes about five minutes so remember to be gentle and always brush towards the heart. Dry brushing boosts the flow of the lymphatic system and improves circulation as well as removes dead skin cells from the surface of the skin.

DRY-BRUSHING STEPS

- Before you start, make sure the brush is completely clean. Beginning with your right leg, place the brush on the top of your right foot. Make small counterclockwise circular motions all over the foot before gradually moving up your right leg. Then repeat on the left leg and foot.
- Next, beginning at your right hand, make small, counterclockwise circular motions over your hand and fingers and all the way up your right arm. Stop when you reach your right shoulder, then repeat on your left.
- Start on the lower left of your stomach, make small, counterclockwise movements with the brush in a counterclockwise circle around your belly button. Move up your stomach to your chest, making circular movements, and brush your chest, moving upward until you reach your neck.
- Rinse off any dead skin cells with a warm shower.

Bonus: Visit a massage therapist on Days 1 and 3 of your detox. Massage speeds up the detoxifying process by increasing circulation and supporting the lymphatic system.

6. Journal each day about your detox experience. Jot down observations in a notebook or journal to document any reflections: how you feel before, during, and after you eat a certain food or how emotionally attached you are to that food or anything that tends to mask your true self. Journaling heightens your awareness and transforms your relationship with food. I promise your detox will be an eye-opening experience, especially when it comes to uncovering patterns of emotional eating and pinpointing allergies. It's a good idea to start journaling the week before your detox so you begin to understand your food choices. A beneficial practice is to write "morning pages" (although you can do them at night; choose what suits you best). These "morning pages" are adapted from Julia Cameron's *The Artist's Way*. You can write three pages in your journal. It can be about anything: thoughts of the day, struggles, wins or brags, your experience. You can also mention three to five things you are grateful for in your life to these writings.

7. It's suggested (but not required) that you take the following supplements during the detox:

- Multivitamin
- Essential fatty acids (omega-3; flax oil)
- B-complex vitamins (make sure to get B12 if you are vegan)
- Magnesium and calcium

- Probiotics
- Vitamin D

Use the recommended dosage for each supplement and consult your doctor if you're taking any medication that might cause a contraindication.

8. Move your body. During your cleanse, be sure to exercise regularly. You should be able to keep up with your routine if you have one or start a habit if you wish.

Just remember to listen to your body. You are detoxing; your body is busy working to "clean house," so take it easy. Check in with your body; modify your workouts if needed, or take walks instead of a run this week. Keep in mind that during detox, it's important to not put undue stress on your body by undertaking a grueling exercise regime. Remember: stress increases inflammation, which is something we want to avoid.

So while you are detoxing, move that cute body of yours . . . even if it's just ten minutes of stretching (which, by the way, is perfect for releasing toxins).

9. Pay attention to your skin. The skin is the largest organ of our body. While you are detoxing with food, don't slather harmful lotions on your skin or expose yourself to sprays and perfumes that have dyes and other toxins that can seep into your pores. Learn about safe and unsafe cosmetics through the Environmental Working Group's Skin Deep cosmetics database: www.ewg.org/skindeep/.

CHAPTER 4

Spring Detox Plan

Each year, spring seems to sneak up on me. I can distinctly remember times where I was shocked to find out that the spring season was in full bloom. The weather would be cold and then, bam, springtime! But the whole time, my body was stirring underneath, ready for something new.

The first time I truly took note of the seasonal shift was way back in college at the University of Pittsburgh. After enduring bitter, frigid, snowy winter months, I slipped on a light jacket to walk to my afternoon psychology class. The sun was beating down on me, and there was just a slight chill in the air. I passed by groups of people scattered on the lawn around the Cathedral of Learning, tossing Frisbees, playing tag football, stretching out on their blankets, reading a book, or sharing lunch. My friends called out to me to join them. So tempting!

Health Focus: LIGHTENING UP

Everything during this time of year is fresh, light and green, and that's how you need to be eating. Dark leafy greens not only reflect the active qualities of spring but also tonify the liver, the spring's primary organ.

Detoxing during spring makes it easier to purge toxins that accumulated during winter. Lightening the body's toxic load can give you tons of energy as well as connect you to the rhythm of spring.

The liver rules over spring and is the body's master laboratory. The liver stores and distributes nourishment for the body and filters toxins from the blood. The liver is also the seat of metabolism, helping to keep blood sugar stable as well as breaking down toxins for elimination.

When you are in balance during spring: new beginnings, cleaning clutter, elimination, greens, creativity, and enthusiasm.

If there are imbalances: laziness, clutter, overeating, excess, boredom.

In fact, I *did* join them: skipped class (yes, I have to tell the truth!), took off my shoes, and wriggled my toes in the grass. Looking around, smiling, and knowing in my heart that change was a-comin', and filled with inspiration and the power to make changes . . . always so exciting.

This season is also the time for spring cleaning. Your body is ready for action. After resting all winter, you now have the energy to clear clutter within your body, your mind, even your home. And a few spring seasons ago, I sure felt the urge to purge. I was in tears all morning, feeling overwhelmed and weighed down with being stuck. To be honest, it felt like I wanted to jump out of my skin. I was irritated and couldn't think clearly.

After I let it all out, had a pep talk from a good friend, and picked myself up, I got to thinking. Spring is a time to get out and move. It's a rebirth. I was excited for so many things that season, but I still felt paralyzed for some reason.

Why?

Well, I realized that way, way down in my basement, there was a huge mess. We had a flood in the laundry room, which damaged tons of toys, holiday decorations, and carpet. Crap was everywhere. So one day, the family and I cleaned and got rid of a lot of junk. We donated toys that didn't get damaged and dropped the yucky stuff in the dump. But we still had a corner filled with leftover crap, just sitting there.

I'm a huge feng shui believer. I know that clutter is connected to our health. Clutter messes with the mind. There are additional reasons why I had a tough morning (you know, life stuff) on that particular day, but I realized that clutter keeps me stuck, uncertain, and irritated. It just adds to the problem. And since the clutter was underneath me, it built and built.

Just like your home, your body needs to be cleared of clutter. A good cleaning from the inside out can make a world of difference in your energy levels as well as your ability to form healthy choices.

Clutter is directly related to weight gain, feeling drained, and cravings.

If your pantry is organized with whole foods instead of half-opened boxes of processed foods, you're more likely to cook healthier meals or grab fruits and veggies for snacks.

Cleansing our bodies with the leafy greens, peas, and strawberries—the spring seasonal foods—while also creating healthy practices for the mind and spirit will help ease you into clearing your clutter. That way, you can open up space for something new and get rid of things that don't serve you anymore.

Spring is the season of beginning, of creation. It's a special time to be open to the new, and to clear out the past which is ready to leave.

What would you like to create? Get rid of? How will you clear away the clutter?

Whether it's getting rid of clothes you haven't worn in five years, eating out less often, starting a meditation practice, or shedding those last few pounds before the pool opens, cleansing can help you create the changes you desire.

By the way, we finally cleaned up our basement . . . such relief and clarity!

Spring Menu Plan

SEASONAL SPRING FOODS*

Arugula, asparagus, chard, dandelion greens, peas, spinach, watercress

Apricots, strawberries

Chives, dill, mint, parsley

*For most who live in temperate climates

	Breakfast	Midmorning Snack	Lunch	Midafternoon Snack	Dinner
DAY 1	Strawberry Silk Smoothie	1 apple with 1 tablespoon raw almond butter	Spring Clean Salad	carrots and celery sticks with White Bean Dip	Feeling Light Soup
DAY 2	Bright and Shiny Smoothie	cucumber slices with Hummus	Pump Up the Iron Salad	grapes (1 cup)	Soul-Full Quinoa
DAY 3	GM Gluten-Free Oatmeal	Tangy Beet Juice	Fancy Arugula Salad	carrots and celery sticks with White Bean Dip	Lean Up Soup
DAY 4	Energy Boost Smoothie	1 apple with 1 tablespoon raw almond butter	Black Beans and Greens	cucumber slices with Hummus	Spicy Asparagus Soup
DAY 5	Coconut Berry Quinoa	Love Your Liver Juice	Chickpea Salad	grapes (1 cup)	Spring Renewal Stuffed Peppers

	Breakfast	Midmorning Snack	Lunch	Midafternoon Snack	Dinner
DAY 6	Strawberry Silk Smoothie	1 apple with 1 tablespoon raw almond butter	Spring Clean Salad	carrots and celery sticks with White Bean Dip	Feeling Light Soup
DAY 7	Bright and Shiny Smoothie	cucumber slices with Hummus	Pump Up the Iron Salad	grapes (1 cup)	Soul-Full Quinoa
DAY 8	GM Gluten-Free Oatmeal	Tangy Beet Juice	Fancy Arugula Salad	carrots and celery sticks with White Bean Dip	Lean Up Soup
DAY 9	Energy Boost Smoothie	1 apple with 1 tablespoon raw almond butter	Black Beans and Greens	cucumber slices with Hummus	Spicy Asparagus Soup
DAY 10	Coconut Berry Quinoa	Love Your Liver Juice	Chickpea Salad	grapes (1 cup)	Spring Renewal Stuffed Peppers

SHOPPING LIST

Greens

- ❑ 4 bunches spinach
- ❑ 3 bunches kale
- ❑ 3 bunches arugula
- ❑ 2 bunches Swiss chard
- ❑ 2 bunches dandelion greens

Vegetables

- ❑ 1–2 bags carrots
- ❑ 1 bag celery
- ❑ 2 cucumbers
- ❑ 2 leeks
- ❑ 2 red bell peppers
- ❑ 3–4 yellow onions
- ❑ 2 parsnips
- ❑ 16 cremini mushrooms
- ❑ 4 beets (with stems)
- ❑ 8–10 radishes
- ❑ 2 pounds asparagus
- ❑ ½ pound fresh peas (or 1 bag frozen peas)
- ❑ 1 package frozen broccoli florets

Fresh Herbs

- ❑ Basil
- ❑ Cilantro
- ❑ Dill
- ❑ Mint
- ❑ Parsley
- ❑ Thyme

Staples

- ❑ Celtic sea salt
- ❑ Freshly ground pepper
- ❑ Extra virgin olive oil
- ❑ 1 garlic bulb
- ❑ Apple cider vinegar
- ❑ Finely ground flaxseeds

Grains

- ❑ 1 bag quinoa (14 ounces)
- ❑ 1 bag gluten-free rolled oats (16 ounces)

Fruits

- ❑ 4 avocados
- ❑ 4 bananas
- ❑ 1 Ruby Red grapefruit
- ❑ 6 apples
- ❑ 2 cartons strawberries
- ❑ 2 mangoes or 1 package frozen mango
- ❑ 4 oranges
- ❑ 1 bunch grapes (green or red)
- ❑ 1 bag lemons

Shelf Items

- ❑ Raw nuts and seeds (avoid salted, roasted)
  Suggest 1 bag each: sunflower seeds, pumpkin seeds, chopped walnuts, pine nuts, cashews, and pecans

- ❏ 1 bag green lentils (or 8 ounces from bulk section)
- ❏ 1 bag red lentils (or 16 ounces from bulk section)
- ❏ 1 8-ounce jar raw almond butter
- ❏ 3 15-ounce cans cannellini beans
- ❏ 2 15-ounce cans black beans
- ❏ 3 15-ounce cans chickpeas
- ❏ Raisins (unsweetened, natural)

Spices

- ❏ Ground cinnamon
- ❏ Turmeric
- ❏ Red pepper flakes
- ❏ Cayenne pepper
- ❏ Fresh gingerroot

Additional Items

- ❏ 1 32-ounce carton almond milk (unsweetened, original)
- ❏ 4 16-ounce cans coconut milk (unsweetened and light)
- ❏ 1 jar tahini (found in nut butter aisle)
- ❏ 2 32-ounce cartons vegetable broth
- ❏ 1 bottle lemon juice
- ❏ 1 bottle lime juice
- ❏ 1 bottle Dijon mustard
- ❏ 1 package coconut flakes (unsweetened)

Coconut Berry Quinoa

serves 1

1 cup cooked quinoa (make ahead of time according to package directions)
½ cup strawberries
1 tablespoon coconut flakes
1 tablespoon pecans
1 teaspoon ground cinnamon

Mix all ingredients in a bowl. Serve.

GM Gluten-Free Oatmeal

serves 1

1 cup cooked gluten-free rolled oats (make ahead of time according to package directions)

¼ cup chopped walnuts

1 tablespoon ground flaxseeds

1 teaspoon ground cinnamon

1 tablespoon raisins

Mix all ingredients in a bowl. Serve.

Spring Clean Salad

serves 1

SALAD

1 bunch kale (1 cup leaves)

1 tablespoon pine nuts

½ Ruby Red grapefruit, peeled, segmented, and membrane removed

½ avocado, peeled, pitted, and cubed

Sea salt and freshly ground pepper to taste

DRESSING

2 tablespoons lemon juice

1 teaspoon Dijon mustard

1 teaspoon chopped mint

1 teaspoon chopped dill

1 tablespoon extra virgin olive oil

Make dressing: Combine juice, mustard, mint, and dill in a small jar and shake well. Add oil and shake well again.

Toss kale with dressing in bowl. Massage kale in dressing. Add pine nuts and toss to combine. Place on plate. Heap grapefruit segments and avocado chunks on top of kale. Drizzle with any remaining dressing. Season with salt and pepper. Serve.

Chickpea Salad

serves 1–2

3 tablespoons pumpkin seeds

1 15-ounce can chickpeas, drained and rinsed

½ cup peas (fresh or frozen)

1 tablespoon chopped basil

1 tablespoon chopped dill

1 tablespoon chopped cilantro

2 tablespoons lemon juice

1 tablespoon extra virgin olive oil

Sea salt and freshly ground pepper to taste

Preheat oven to 350°F. Place pumpkin seeds on baking tray. Bake for 3 to 5 minutes. Set aside to cool.

In a large bowl, combine chickpeas, peas, and herbs. Add cooled seeds to mixture and stir in juice and oil. Season with salt and pepper. Toss and serve.

Black Beans and Greens

serves 1–2

1 15-ounce can black beans, drained and rinsed
½ mango, peeled, pitted and cubed (½ cup)
½ avocado, peeled, pitted, and cubed
1 tablespoon extra virgin olive oil
1 tablespoon lime juice
1 bunch spinach (1 cup leaves)
1 tablespoon chopped cilantro
Sea salt and freshly ground pepper to taste

In a bowl, toss together beans, mango, avocado, oil, and juice. Pour over a bed of spinach. Sprinkle cilantro on top. Season with salt and pepper. Serve.

Fancy Arugula Salad

serves 1

1 bunch arugula (1 cup leaves)
½ cup radishes, chopped
½ cup asparagus, chopped
½ onion, chopped (1/4 cup)
1 tablespoon sunflower seeds
1 tablespoon lemon juice
1 tablespoon extra virgin olive oil

Toss all ingredients in a bowl and serve.

Pump Up the Iron Salad

serves 1

SALAD
1 bunch dandelion greens (1 cup leaves)
½ cup cooked green lentils (make ahead of time according to package directions)
2 tablespoons pumpkin seeds

DRESSING
1 tablespoon extra virgin olive oil
1 garlic clove, minced
1 tablespoon lemon juice
½ avocado, peeled, pitted, and cubed
Sea salt and freshly ground pepper to taste

Combine salad ingredients in a large bowl.

Make dressing: Blend all dressing ingredients in food processor.

Toss dressing over salad and mix well. Season with salt and pepper. Serve.

Lean Up Soup

serves 1–2

1 tablespoon extra virgin olive oil
1 garlic clove, minced
½ onion, chopped (¼ cup)
1-inch piece fresh gingerroot, peeled and chopped
1 cup broccoli florets
1 bunch spinach (1 cup leaves)
1 parsnip, peeled, cored, chopped (½ cup)
2 celery stalks, chopped (¼ cup)
1 tablespoon chopped parsley
2 cups vegetable broth
1 tablespoon lemon juice
Sea salt and freshly ground pepper to taste

In a large pot, heat oil over medium heat. Add garlic, onion, and ginger and cook for 2 minutes. Add broccoli, spinach, parsnip, celery, and parsley. Cook for 5 to 7 minutes. Add vegetable broth and reduce heat to medium-low. Cover the pot and simmer for 10 minutes. Add juice and purée the soup in a blender. Pour soup into bowl. Season with salt and pepper. Serve.

Optional: Add 1 cup coconut milk to make it even creamier.

Spring Renewal Stuffed Peppers *serves 1*

1 red bell pepper, seeded and halved (½ cup)
1 tablespoon extra virgin olive oil
½ onion, chopped (¼ cup)
1 cup red lentils, rinsed and drained
1 cup water
2 carrots, finely diced (¼ cup)
1 tablespoon raisins
1 tablespoon cashews, chopped
Sea salt to taste

Preheat oven to 350°F. Place peppers cut side down in baking dish. Cover with foil and bake for 10 minutes. Set aside.

Meanwhile, heat oil in large saucepan over medium heat. Add onion and sauté for 2 minutes. Stir in lentils and water. Add carrot and raisins. Cover and bring to boil. Reduce heat to low and simmer for 10 minutes. Remove from heat and stir in nuts. Season with salt.

Flip peppers. Fill each with lentil mixture. Re-cover baking dish and bake for 5 to 7 minutes. Remove from oven and serve.

Spicy Asparagus Soup

serves 1–2

2 cups vegetable broth, divided
1 tablespoon cashews
2 cups asparagus, chopped
1 garlic clove, peeled
½ onion, sliced (¼ cup)
1 teaspoon red pepper flakes
Sea salt to taste

In a blender, combine ½ cup of the broth with cashews until smooth. Add asparagus, garlic, onion, and remaining 1½ cups broth to the blender. Blend on high until perfectly smooth. Pour the soup into a saucepan and heat until hot, stirring frequently. Season with pepper flakes and salt. Serve.

Soul-Full Quinoa

serves 1–2

1 tablespoon extra virgin olive oil
1 garlic clove, minced
1 teaspoon chopped thyme
8 cremini mushrooms, sliced
1 cup cooked quinoa (make ahead of time according to package directions)
1 bunch arugula (1 cup leaves)
Sea salt and freshly ground pepper to taste

Heat oil in a large saucepan over medium-high heat. Add garlic and thyme and cook for 1 minute. Add mushrooms and cook for 5 minutes. Transfer mushroom mixture to a bowl and stir in quinoa and arugula. Toss and season with salt and pepper. Serve.

Feeling Light Soup

1 garlic clove, minced

2 tablespoons extra virgin olive oil, divided

1 leek (white part only), chopped crosswise (1 cup)

1 15-ounce can cannellini beans, rinsed and drained

1 bunch Swiss chard, chopped (1 cup leaves)

2 cups vegetable broth

Sea salt and freshly ground pepper to taste

Place a large pot over medium heat and sauté garlic in 1 tablespoon of the oil for 2 minutes. Add leek and beans, stirring to combine. Cook for 10 minutes. Stir in chard and remaining 1 tablespoon oil and cook for 5 minutes. Add broth and cook for 10 minutes. Season with salt and pepper and serve.

Smoothies

Strawberry Silk Smoothie

Makes approximately 18 ounces

2 cups almond milk
1 bunch kale (1 cup leaves)
½ avocado, peeled and pitted
½ cup strawberries

Blend all ingredients and serve.

Bright and Shiny Smoothie

Makes approximately 18 ounces

2 cups coconut milk
1 orange, peeled and segmented
1 banana
1 teaspoon turmeric

Blend all ingredients and serve.

Energy Boost Smoothie

Makes approximately 18 ounces

2 cups coconut milk
1 bunch spinach (1 cup leaves)
1 banana
½ cup mango
1 tablespoon raw almond butter
1 tablespoon ground flaxseeds

Blend all ingredients and serve.

Tangy Beet Juice

Makes approximately 12 ounces

2 beets, chopped into chunks
3–4 carrots
1 orange, peeled and segmented
½ lemon, peeled
¼-inch piece fresh gingerroot, peeled

Juice the ingredients and serve.

Love Your Liver Juice

Makes approximately 12 ounces

1 bunch spinach (1 cup leaves)
2–4 celery stalks
1 apple, cored
½ lemon, peeled
Dash of cayenne pepper

Juice the ingredients and serve.

White Bean Dip

serves 4

1 15-ounce can cannellini beans, rinsed and drained
1 tablespoon extra virgin olive oil
1 garlic clove, minced
½ onion, chopped (¼ cup)
Sea salt to taste

In food processor, blend all ingredients except salt. Add water as needed, 1 tablespoon at a time, to create a smooth consistency. Season with salt.

Note: If kept in airtight glass container in the fridge, the dip will last for 4 to 5 days.

Hummus

serves 4

1 15-ounce can chickpeas, rinsed and drained
1 tablespoon extra virgin olive oil
1 garlic clove, minced
½ cup tahini
1 tablespoon lemon juice
Sea salt to taste

In a blender, combine all ingredients except salt. Add water as needed, 1 tablespoon at a time, to create a smooth consistency. Season with salt.

Note: If kept in an airtight glass container in the fridge, the hummus will last for 4 to 5 days.

CHAPTER 5

Summer Detox Plan

Bodies moving slow but days flying by. As night falls, catching lightning bugs in glass jars; the sound of punching holes through the lids before screwing them on tight. Carnivals at the local fire station. And thunderstorms. Summer, ahhhh, summer.

Even though I couldn't wait for school to start after a month or two of summer vacation (the usual kid feeling: "There's nothing to do, I'm bored"), I never got enough of one more opportunity to sit on the back porch with my dad, shooting the breeze while the wind kicked up a good storm and we watched lightning grace the sky.

The last summer I did that was thirty years ago, but I remember like it happened today. At one clap of thunder, I would race downstairs and jump on the porch swing. My dad would already be waiting for me, and we would sit, talk, and sit some more during these storms. A lot of the times we were simply silent, witnessing the beauty of nature's light show.

When we did talk, topics ranged from what happened during his workday to what happened on the playground with my sister to, well, all kinds of life things. I remember feeling so close to my dad then, that we shared a special ritual just between us.

All my senses were engaged as the storm rolled out and the after-storm treats rolled in.

The steam rising off the pavement . . .

Green and lush plants and flowers . . .

The sweet, clean smell of the air . . .

What summer treasures do you hold tight in your heart and revisit in your mind? What rituals have you created?

It's true, in summer we slow down with work and the busy life and focus more on play. But oddly in contrast to that slowing down, summer is actually a very active time of year. We might reduce our workload, submit to the vacation schedules of others, and abandon big plans for "slow month" achievements. But in fact, summer represents energy and lots of movement. This energy leads to recharging with lots of playtime which encourages us to think of our lives in a special way.

Summer is the season of growth. Lush trees flank the streets. Flowers and fruits are abundant and gardens are flourishing. My garden typically resembles a jungle!

As nature matures, we also thrive by being outside, especially swimming and hiking. We should view this growth with the same importance we consider our work and goals. These activities—the desire to get out and move our bodies, to stay awake to capture one last lightning bug, to take one last dip in the pool—should be revered and cherished, perhaps even ritualized in some way.

In addition to appreciating the benefits of summertime movement and long days, it's important that we feed our bodies and, in conjunction, feed our souls. During the hot months, we need food that keeps us cool and light. Isn't it lovely that nature provides abundant fruits and veggies in summer? Raw food is extremely nourishing this time of year.

Summer is ruled by the heart. I don't think it's a coincidence that my memories of summer are tightly tethered to matters of my heart: my special time with my dad.

As I've grown up, as my children develop, I find that we have developed rituals that mark summer in different ways—such as taking the afternoons off to head to the pool with packed lunches and a few tagalong friends. I let go of work I have to do and just sit in the sun (with nontoxic sunscreen, of course!), do laps, and laugh with the kids at all the fun they are having splashing around.

Health Focus: COOLING AND HYDRATION

Your body is hot and dry during summer so balance your system with cool, juicy foods like melons and cucumbers. Summer is governed by the heart and small intestine according to Traditional Chinese Medicine; therefore, you'll need to eat foods that support these organs. Fruits, veggies, juices and smoothies will do the trick. You'll want to eat lighter and cook as little as possible. Raw foods are ideal.

The heart, ruler over summer, is the source of vitality and provides clarity as well as helping you serve with love.

The small intestine is the secondary organ governing the summer months. The small intestine functions to receive, digest, and process nourishment. It sorts out and extracts the good from what we ingest, physically as well as emotionally.

When you are in balance during summer: energy, intense exercise and movement, good times, play, vacation, eating light.

If there are imbalances: shy, over serious, going within and staying inside, lack of courage, fearful.

I've also found that nutrition has become a cornerstone of my family's summer life. Some of our rituals developed around healthy food habits. My kids and I use the nonschool time to head to farmers' markets. I step back and let them select the fruits that interest them the most. Their little hands closing around a fresh peach, the smile on Kate's face as she excitedly describes how we will use the fruit to make a pie or frozen fruit bars . . . these sweet moments tug at my heart and bring the feeling of that special time with my dad back to the here and now.

Summer Menu Plan

SEASONAL SUMMER FOODS*

Cauliflower, celery, corn, cucumbers, eggplant, fennel, oyster mushrooms, peas, bell and chili peppers, summer squash, tomatoes, zucchini

Blueberries, cherries, melons, nectarines, peaches, plums, raspberries, watermelon

Basil, lemon verbena, rosemary, sage, thyme

*For most who live in temperate climates

	Breakfast	Midmorning Snack	Lunch	Midafternoon Snack	Dinner
DAY 1	Pineapple Spinach Smoothie	frozen green grapes (1 cup) with almonds on top (1–2 ounces)	Avocado Tomato Salad with Hot Stuff Dressing	carrot sticks and red bell peppers with 1 tablespoon tahini	Mushroom Sliders
DAY 2	Warrior Juice *or* Crunch Cereal	Kale Chips with a Kick! (1–2 servings)	Peachy Arugula Salad	cherries (1 cup)	Squash Surprise with Pesto
DAY 3	Mango Chia Smoothie	strawberries (1 cup) with raw nuts and seeds on top (1–2 ounces)	Light and Cleansing Salad	cucumber slices and zucchini sticks with Fresh Dip	Taco Salad
DAY 4	Minty Detox Juice *or* Crunch Cereal	carrot sticks and red bell peppers with 1 tablespoon tahini	Melon Soup	1 apple with 1 tablespoon raw almond butter	Ratatouille Supreme

	Breakfast	Midmorning Snack	Lunch	Midafternoon Snack	Dinner
DAY 5	Green Nutty Buddy Smoothie	cucumber slices and zucchini sticks with Fresh Dip (1 serving)	Fresh Herb Mango Salad	strawberries (1 cup) with raw nuts and seeds on top (1–2 ounces)	Raw Tabbouleh
DAY 6	Drink Your Veggies Juice *or* Crunch Cereal	cherries (1 cup)	Powerhouse Salad	Kale Chips with a Kick! (1–2 servings)	Creamy Avocado and Cucumber Soup
DAY 7	Silky Berry Smoothie	1 apple with 1 tablespoon raw almond butter	"Cheesy" Kale Salad	frozen green grapes (1 cup) with almonds on top (1–2 ounces)	Chilled Tomato Soup

Note: For snacks and any meals, you can eat as many veggies as you like. ☺

SHOPPING LIST

Greens
- ❏ 4 bunches spinach
- ❏ 1 bunch arugula
- ❏ 3 bunches kale
- ❏ 1 bag mixed greens

Vegetables
- ❏ 1 carton cherry tomatoes
- ❏ 6 tomatoes (Roma preferred)
- ❏ 3–4 red bell peppers
- ❏ 1 green bell pepper
- ❏ 2 yellow onions
- ❏ 1 eggplant
- ❏ 3 zucchini
- ❏ 1 yellow squash
- ❏ 1 bag celery
- ❏ 1 bag carrots
- ❏ 6–7 cucumbers
- ❏ 2 portobello mushrooms
- ❏ 1 bag frozen cauliflower florets
- ❏ 1 package frozen broccoli florets

Fresh Herbs
- ❏ Cilantro
- ❏ Parsley
- ❏ Basil
- ❏ Chives
- ❏ Mint

Staples
- ❏ Celtic sea salt
- ❏ Freshly ground pepper
- ❏ Extra virgin olive oil
- ❏ 1 garlic bulb
- ❏ Apple cider vinegar
- ❏ Finely ground flaxseeds

Fruits
- ❏ 1 peach
- ❏ 2 mangoes or 1 bag frozen mango
- ❏ 1 pineapple (or 1 bag frozen pineapple chunks)
- ❏ 1 carton blueberries
- ❏ 1 carton strawberries
- ❏ 1 bunch green grapes
- ❏ 1 bag cherries
- ❏ 3 apples
- ❏ 1 Ruby Red grapefruit
- ❏ 1 small watermelon
- ❏ 1 banana
- ❏ 5 avocados
- ❏ 1 bag lemons
- ❏ 1 lime

Shelf Items
- ❏ Raw nuts and seeds (avoid salted, roasted) Suggest 1 bag each: sunflower seeds, pumpkin seeds, chopped walnuts, almonds, pine nuts, cashews, and pecans

- ❑ 1 8-ounce jar raw almond butter
- ❑ 1 15-ounce can chickpeas
- ❑ Dried cranberries (unsweetened, natural)

- ❑ 1 bottle lemon juice
- ❑ 1 bottle lime juice
- ❑ 1 jar tahini (found in nut butter aisle)
- ❑ 1 bottle red wine vinegar
- ❑ 1 bottle balsamic vinegar

Spices

- ❑ Paprika
- ❑ Cumin
- ❑ Cayenne pepper
- ❑ Chili powder
- ❑ Red pepper flakes
- ❑ Ground cinnamon

Superfood Additions

- ❑ 1 package hemp seeds
- ❑ 1 package chia seeds
- ❑ 8 ounces nutritional yeast (find in bulk/pantry)
- ❑ Spirulina (optional)
- ❑ Maca powder (optional)

Additional Items

- ❑ 1 32-ounce carton almond milk (unsweetened, original)
- ❑ 2 16-ounce cans coconut milk (unsweetened, light)

Breakfast

See Smoothie and Juice recipes (on pages 101–104). If you don't have a juicer or have a juice shop nearby, then you can substitute Crunch Cereal.

Crunch Cereal
serves 1

1 apple, chopped
1 tablespoon chopped walnuts
1 tablespoon almonds
½ tablespoon raisins
½ tablespoon pumpkin seeds
½ tablespoon ground flaxseeds
½ tablespoon hemp seeds
½ cup almond milk

Mix all dry ingredients in bowl. Pour almond milk on top. Serve.

Note: If you substitute this meal, don't forget to add the extra ingredients to your shopping list! The shopping list only includes items for the main menu. ☺

Avocado Tomato Salad with Hot Stuff Dressing

serves 1

SALAD

1 cup cherry tomatoes, halved

1 bunch spinach (1 cup leaves)

½ avocado, peeled, pitted and cubed

1 tablespoon chopped cilantro

1 tablespoon chopped parsley

1 tablespoon pumpkin seeds

Sea salt and freshly ground pepper to taste

DRESSING

3 tablespoons cashews

1 red bell pepper, seeded and chopped (½ cup)

1 teaspoon paprika

½ onion, chopped (¼ cup)

1 tablespoon lemon juice

Make dressing: Soak cashews in bowl of cold water for 30 minutes, then drain and put in blender or food processor. Add rest of dressing ingredients and process until creamy.

Combine tomatoes, spinach, avocado, cilantro, and parsley in a bowl and toss with dressing. Top with pumpkin seeds. Season with salt and pepper. Serve.

Peachy Arugula Salad

serves 1

SALAD
1 bunch arugula (1 cup leaves)
1 peach, pitted and thinly sliced
1 green bell pepper, chopped (½ cup)
1 tablespoon almonds

DRESSING
1 tablespoon extra virgin olive oil
1 tablespoon balsamic vinegar
1 tablespoon lemon juice
Sea salt to taste

Combine arugula, peach, pepper, and almonds in a large bowl.

Make dressing: Whisk together oil, vinegar, and juice in small bowl.

Toss salad with dressing. Season with salt. Serve.

Melon Soup

serves 1

1 tablespoon extra virgin olive oil
1 tomato, chopped (½ cup)
2 cups watermelon, seeded and cut into ½-inch cubes
1 cucumber, peeled
1 tablespoon lime juice
1 tablespoon chopped cilantro
Sea salt and freshly ground pepper to taste

Blend all ingredients in blender or food processor. Chill in fridge for 15 minutes before serving. Season with salt and pepper. Serve.

Light and Cleansing Salad

serves 1

SALAD
1 bunch spinach (1 cup leaves)
1 Ruby Red grapefruit, peeled, segmented, and membranes removed
1 avocado, peeled, pitted, and sliced
1 tablespoon sunflower seeds
Sea salt and freshly ground pepper to taste

DRESSING
2 tablespoons red wine vinegar
1 tablespoon extra virgin olive oil

In a large bowl, combine spinach, grapefruit, and avocado.

Make dressing: Whisk vinegar and oil in a small bowl.

Toss salad with dressing and top with seeds. Season with salt and pepper. Serve.

Powerhouse Salad

serves 1

1 cup broccoli florets
1 cup cauliflower florets
1 tablespoon raisins
1 tablespoon sunflower seeds
1 tablespoon lemon juice
Sea salt and freshly ground pepper to taste

In blender or food processor, pulse broccoli and cauliflower until fine. Do the same with cauliflower. Add to a large bowl. Add raisins, seeds, and juice and toss together. Season with salt and pepper. Serve.

Fresh Herb Mango Salad

serves 1

SALAD
1 mango, peeled, pitted, and thinly sliced
1 avocado, peeled, pitted, and thinly sliced
1 tablespoon chopped basil

DRESSING
1 tablespoon extra virgin olive oil
1 tablespoon balsamic vinegar
1 tablespoon lime juice
Sea salt and freshly ground pepper to taste

In a large bowl, combine mango, avocado, and basil.

Make dressing: Whisk together dressing ingredients in a small bowl.

Season with salt and pepper. Pour over salad and toss. Serve.

"Cheesy" Kale Salad

serves 1–2

SALAD
1 bunch kale, stems removed and chopped (1 cup leaves)
1 garlic clove, minced
1 tablespoon lemon juice
1 tablespoon extra virgin olive oil
Sea salt and freshly ground pepper to taste
1 tablespoon dried cranberries

"CHEESE"
½ cup pecans
1 tablespoon nutritional yeast
1 tablespoon extra virgin olive oil

Place kale in a large bowl.

In a blender or food processor, combine the garlic, juice, oil, and salt and pepper until combined. Pour dressing onto kale and mix together, tossing continuously for 1 to 2 minutes.

Make "cheese": In a blender or food processor, add pecans, nutritional yeast, and oil and process until crunchy and coarse in texture.

Sprinkle "cheese" on kale and top with cranberries. Serve.

Chilled Tomato Soup

serves 1

3 tomatoes

1 cup coconut milk

1 tablespoon extra virgin olive oil

½ onion, chopped (¼ cup)

1 red bell pepper, seeded and chopped (½ cup)

1 tablespoon lime juice

½ teaspoon cumin

In a blender or food processor, purée all ingredients until smooth. Chill in fridge for 15 minutes. Serve.

Mushroom Sliders

serves 1–2

2 portobello mushrooms, stemmed and gilled
1 tablespoon extra virgin olive oil
1 tablespoon apple cider vinegar

"CHEESE"
2 cups cashews
½ cup water
2 tablespoons nutritional yeast
1 tablespoon lemon juice
1 garlic clove

TOPPINGS
1 tomato, sliced (½ cup)
1 bunch spinach (1 cup leaves)
1 tablespoon chopped chives

Coat mushrooms with oil and vinegar and marinate in a small bowl for 10 minutes.

Make "cheese": Blend all "cheese" ingredients in a food processor until smooth. Adjust ingredients accordingly so that the mixture is thick. Let sit for 10 minutes.

Drain the marinade from the mushrooms, and then spread "cheese" onto mushrooms and layer with tomatoes, spinach, and chives. Serve.

Ratatouille Supreme

serves 1

1 eggplant, cut into large chunks (1 cup)
1 zucchini, cut into large chunks (½ cup)
1 tomato, chopped (½ cup)
1 red bell pepper, seeded and sliced (½ cup)
1 garlic clove, minced
½ onion, sliced (¼ cup)
1 tablespoon extra virgin olive oil
1 tablespoon lemon juice
Sea salt and freshly ground pepper to taste

Combine all ingredients in a large bowl and toss. Serve.

Creamy Avocado and Cucumber Soup

serves 1

2 cucumbers, peeled, seeded, and chopped
1 avocado, peeled, pitted, and chopped
1 tablespoon lime juice
½ teaspoon red pepper flakes
Sea salt to taste

Purée all ingredients in a blender or food processor until smooth and creamy. Serve.

Raw Tabbouleh

SALAD
1 cup cauliflower florets
2 celery stalks, chopped (¼ cup)
1 tablespoon minced cilantro
1 tablespoon hemp seeds

DRESSING
1 tablespoon red wine vinegar
1 tablespoon extra virgin olive oil
½ tablespoon ground flaxseeds
Sea salt to taste

Grate cauliflower in blender or food processor. Place in large bowl. Add celery, cilantro, and hemp seeds and toss together.

Make dressing: Whisk together vinegar, olive oil, and flaxseeds. Season with salt.

Add to salad and toss to combine. Serve.

Pineapple Spinach Smoothie

Makes approximately 18 ounces

2 cups coconut milk
1 bunch spinach (1 cup leaves)
½ banana
¼ cup frozen or fresh pineapple chunks
1 tablespoon hemp seeds

Blend all ingredients and serve.

Optional: Add 1 tablespoon maca powder for superfood boost.

Mango Chia Smoothie

Makes approximately 18 ounces

2 cups almond milk
½ mango, pitted and peeled (½ cup)
1 tablespoon lime juice
2 tablespoons chia seeds

Blend all ingredients and serve.

Optional: Add 1 tablespoon spirulina for superfood boost.

Silk Berry Smoothie

Makes approximately 18 ounces

2 cups coconut milk
1 bunch kale (1 cup leaves)
½ avocado, peeled and pitted
½ cup blueberries
1 tablespoon ground flaxseeds

Blend all ingredients and serve.

Optional: Add 1 tablespoon maca powder for superfood boost.

Green Nutty Buddy Smoothie

Makes approximately 18 ounces

2 cups almond milk
1 bunch spinach (1 cup leaves)
½ banana
1 tablespoon raw almond butter
1 tablespoon ground flaxseeds
1 teaspoon ground cinnamon
¼ cup chopped walnuts

Blend all ingredients except walnuts. Top with nuts and serve.

Optional: Add 1 tablespoon spirulina for superfood boost.

Juices

Minty Detox Juice

Makes approximately 12 ounces

2–3 lemons, peeled
½ cup filtered water
1 tablespoon mint
¼ teaspoon cayenne pepper

Juice the ingredients and serve.

Drink Your Veggies Juice

Makes approximately 12 ounces

½ bunch spinach (½ cup leaves)
1 bunch kale (1 cup leaves)
1 cucumber
1–2 celery stalks
½ lemon, peeled

Juice the ingredients and serve.

Warrior Juice

Makes approximately 12 ounces

1 cucumber
2 carrots
1 apple
1 tablespoon basil
½ lime, peeled

Juice the ingredients and serve.

Kale Chips with a Kick!

serves 1–2

You can experiment with using a dehydrator to make kale chips, or follow this recipe.

1 bunch kale, stems and inner ribs removed (1 cup leaves)
1 tablespoon lime juice
1 tablespoon extra virgin olive oil
2 tablespoons tahini (or raw almond butter)
½ teaspoon red pepper flakes
¼ teaspoon sea salt

Preheat oven to 115°F.

Use a knife to cut out the tough inner rib that runs lengthwise through the center of each kale leaf. Then cut the kale into large pieces.

In a small bowl, whisk together the remaining ingredients. Place the kale in a large bowl and pour the mixture over the kale. Massage the kale with your hands, coating each leaf thoroughly. Distribute the kale pieces evenly on a cookie sheet so they are in one layer.

Bake for about 20 minutes. Flip the leaves about halfway through the baking time, and watch that they don't burn. They should be crisp and dry before serving.

Fresh Dip

serves 4

1 15-ounce can chickpeas, rinsed and drained
1 cucumber
1 garlic clove
2 tablespoons tahini
½ cup water
2 tablespoons lemon juice
1 teaspoon cumin
1 tablespoon ground flaxseeds
Sea salt and freshly ground pepper to taste

In a blender or food processor, blend all ingredients until creamy.

Note: If kept in an airtight glass container in fridge, dip will last for 4–5 days.

DIY Milk Recipes

If you want to make your own milks, please do! Make sure to add any extra ingredients to your shopping list, since these ingredients aren't included in the master list.

DIY ALMOND MILK

Makes 24 ounces

1 cup almonds, soaked overnight (12 hours)
3 cups filtered water
2–3 medjool dates

Blend all ingredients in a blender. If you don't have a high-powered blender, strain the soaked almonds into a large bowl through cheesecloth. Put the mixture into a blender with the dates. Pour into pitcher and keep refrigerated for up to 7 days.

DIY COCONUT MILK

Makes 32 ounces

1 cup coconut cream
1 cup coconut water
2 cups water

Add all ingredients to a large container or pitcher. Stir and keep refrigerated for up to 7 days.

CHAPTER 6

Fall Detox Plan

My absolute favorite time of year is autumn. Hands down. I like everything about the fall season: football, pumpkins, spiced apple drinks, the crisp air smell. Halloween is my favorite holiday.

I can remember when I first really acknowledged how good autumn feels. During my third year of teaching elementary school, I went for a run after work. It was early October, because I can picture the pumpkins and mums on doorsteps. I needed a pullover, which I threw on without really noticing.

All of a sudden, it got dark quickly. I was startled, as I had just begun my usual three-mile routine. I actually said aloud, "Ahhhh, it's now fall!" I began to take in the crunching of the leaves as I ran, the chill in the air, and stillness of the evening.

Fall is the perfect time of year to gather in and prepare your body for the cold and dry winter months. In order to boost immunity, nature takes care of us with beta-carotene rich pumpkin and butternut squash. Not only are they sweet, but these veggies curb sugar cravings and also keep us energized during the shorter days.

We need to protect our lungs, the organ of fall, so that we can set up a strong immune system to ward off flu and colds of winter.

Lungs represent balance within the body as well as vitality and instinct. The rhythm of the breath paces the other cycles in the body such as the heart and blood circulation. Respiration is vital for life therefore the lungs are our basic life force.

When you are in balance during fall: communication, productivity, study, clarity, more rest, quiet.

If there are imbalances: indecision, confusion, fatigue, overindulgence.

I can remember being so happy during that run. Being fully present with my surroundings. Feeling comfort and ease with nature.

Now I make sure to fully take in all that fall has to offer. Hearing the high school marching band practice in the late afternoons. Going apple picking with Jack and Kate. Finding the perfect costume to wear for trick-or-treating.

Also, there's a buzz inside of me during fall. It's actually a very productive time of year, even better than New Year's for making resolutions and starting and following through on projects. You are done with summer debauchery and ready to get back to business. And that feeling of starting over is so strong this time of year. It's actually nature's way of bringing new disciplines and productivity to life.

Can you feel the buzzing energy? It's time. Time to get it done. Whatever your "it" is, fall is the time of year to make sure you follow through.

As a former elementary school teacher for fifteen years, and having attended school for about eighteen years, I find that each autumn a nostalgic feeling of getting another chance, of starting new things, washes over me. Whatever health goal you want to accomplish, now is the time to get moving on it.

- Lose a few pounds and feel good in your clothes.
- Plan healthy meals for you and your family.
- Have more energy to get through the day.
- Limit the sugar because you know it makes you feel like crap.
- Look like a goddess during the holidays.

It's time to receive all the benefits from your work and projects in the last six months.
It's time to prepare for longer, darker nights and to focus more on you.
It's time to get going . . . and finish what you started.

Fall Menu Plan

SEASONAL FALL FOODS*

Brussels sprouts, butternut squash, carrots, garlic, kale, pumpkin

Apples, figs, pears

*For most who live in temperate climates

	Breakfast	Midmorning Snack	Lunch	Midafternoon Snack	Dinner
DAY 1	Pear, Kale, and Almond Smoothie	1 apple with 1 tablespoon raw almond butter	Oh So Good Spinach Salad	carrot sticks and red bell peppers with White Bean Dip**	Lentil Stew
DAY 2	Pumpkin Treat	grapes (1 cup)	Autumn Salad	handful raw nuts and seeds (1–2 ounces)	Kale and Carrot Soup
DAY 3	Apple Pie and Banana Oatmeal	1 apple with 1 tablespoon raw almond butter	White Bean, Beet, and Butternut Salad	cucumber and celery sticks with Hummus**	Creamy Broccoli Soup
DAY 4	Cinnamon Roll Millet	Red Alert Juice	Nectarine and Watercress Salad	carrot sticks and red bell peppers with White Bean Dip**	Roasted Brussels Sprouts with Mixed Baby Greens Salad
DAY 5	Start Me Up Smoothie	cucumber and celery sticks with Hummus	Cleansing Fall Salad	grapes (1 cup)	Sweater Season Soup

**Hummus and White Bean Dip Recipes (see page 79)

	Breakfast	Midmorning Snack	Lunch	Midafternoon Snack	Dinner
DAY 6	Pear, Kale, and Almond Smoothie	1 apple with 1 tablespoon raw almond butter	Oh So Good Spinach Salad	carrot sticks and red bell peppers with White Bean Dip**	Lentil Stew
DAY 7	Pumpkin Treat	grapes (1 cup)	Autumn Salad	handful raw nuts and seeds (1–2 ounces)	Kale and Carrot Soup
DAY 8	Apple Pie and Banana Oatmeal	1 apple with 1 tablespoon raw almond butter	White Bean, Beet, and Butternut Salad	cucumber and celery sticks with Hummus**	Creamy Broccoli Soup
DAY 9	Cinnamon Roll Millet	Red Alert Juice	Nectarine and Watercress Salad	carrot sticks and red bell peppers with White Bean Dip**	Roasted Brussels Sprouts with Mixed Baby Green Salad
DAY 10	Start Me Up Smoothie	cucumber and celery sticks with Hummus	Cleansing Fall Salad	grapes (1 cup)	Sweater Season Soup

SHOPPING LIST

Greens

- ❑ 4 bunches spinach
- ❑ 3 bunches kale
- ❑ 1 bunch Swiss chard
- ❑ 1 bunch watercress
- ❑ 2 bags mixed greens

Vegetables

- ❑ 1 bag carrots
- ❑ 1 bag celery
- ❑ 5 cucumbers
- ❑ 4 red bell peppers
- ❑ 4–5 yellow onions
- ❑ 1 carton cherry tomatoes
- ❑ 6 beets (with stems)
- ❑ 2 butternut squash (or use prepackaged cubes)
- ❑ 2 pounds Brussels sprouts
- ❑ 2 sweet potatoes
- ❑ 1 bag frozen broccoli florets

Fresh and Dried Herbs

- ❑ Dried oregano
- ❑ Basil
- ❑ Cilantro
- ❑ Sage

Staples

- ❑ Celtic sea salt
- ❑ Freshly ground pepper

- ❑ Extra virgin olive oil
- ❑ 1 garlic bulb
- ❑ Apple cider vinegar
- ❑ Finely ground flaxseeds

Grains

- ❑ 1 bag gluten-free rolled oats (16 ounces)
- ❑ 1 bag quinoa (14 ounces)
- ❑ 1 bag millet (28 ounces)

Fruits

- ❑ 4 pears
- ❑ 10 apples
- ❑ 1 bunch grapes (green or red)
- ❑ 3 bananas
- ❑ 4 nectarines
- ❑ 1 carton blueberries
- ❑ 1 bag lemons
- ❑ 1 avocado

Shelf Items

- ❑ Raw nuts and seeds (avoid salted, roasted) Suggest 1 bag each: sunflower seeds, pumpkin seeds, chopped walnuts, cashews, and pecans
- ❑ 1 bag red lentils (or 16 ounces from bulk section)
- ❑ 1 8-ounce jar raw almond butter
- ❑ 1 15-ounce can chickpeas
- ❑ 5 15-ounce cans cannellini beans
- ❑ 2 15-ounce cans diced tomatoes

- ❑ 3 14.5-ounce cans pumpkin purée (100% organic)
- ❑ Raisins (unsweetened, natural)
- ❑ Dried cranberries (unsweetened, natural)

Spices

- ❑ Ground cinnamon
- ❑ Ground cloves
- ❑ Cayenne pepper
- ❑ Pumpkin pie spice
- ❑ Ground allspice
- ❑ Ground nutmeg
- ❑ Cumin
- ❑ Fresh gingerroot

Additional Items

- ❑ 2 32-ounce cartons almond milk (unsweetened, original)
- ❑ 4 16-ounce cans coconut milk (unsweetened, light)
- ❑ 1 jar coconut oil
- ❑ 1 bottle red wine vinegar
- ❑ 1 bottle balsamic vinegar
- ❑ 4 32-ounce cartons vegetable broth
- ❑ 1 jar tahini (found in nut butter aisle)
- ❑ 1 bottle lemon juice

Apple Pie and Banana Oatmeal   *serves 1–2*

1 cup gluten-free rolled oats
1 cup coconut milk
½ apple, peeled, cored, and chopped
½ banana, sliced
¼ teaspoon pumpkin pie spice
¼ teaspoon ground cinnamon
1 tablespoon chopped walnuts

In a medium-size saucepan, cook the oats, milk, and apple over medium heat for 5 minutes. Reduce heat to low and cook for 3 minutes, until apples soften. Stir in banana. Continue to stir until mixture thickens (about 2-3 minutes). Add pumpkin pie spice and cinnamon and stir until combined.

Meanwhile, in a skillet, toast walnuts over low heat for 1 to 2 minutes.

Pour serving of oats mixture in a bowl and top with walnuts. Serve.

Pumpkin Treat

serves 1–2

1 cup cooked quinoa (make ahead of time according to package directions)
¼ cup almond milk
¼ cup pumpkin purée
1 teaspoon coconut oil
½ teaspoon ground cinnamon
½ teaspoon ground nutmeg
1 tablespoon pecans

In a small bowl, combine all ingredients except pecans. Make sure treat is warm and toss pecans on top when ready to serve.

Cinnamon Roll Millet

serves 1–2

1 cup millet, rinsed and drained
1 ½ cups water
1 tablespoon coconut oil
1 teaspoon ground cinnamon
¼ teaspoon ground cloves
½ cup almond milk
1 tablespoon ground flaxseeds

Combine millet, water, oil, cinnamon, and cloves in a large saucepan. Cover and bring to a boil on medium-high heat. Reduce heat to low and cook for 10 minutes.

Add milk and flaxseeds. Stir, cover, and cook for another 5 minutes. Serve.

Oh So Good Spinach Salad

serves 1–2

SALAD
1 bunch spinach (1 cup leaves)
1 pear, cored, quartered, and sliced
1 tablespoon dried cranberries

SPICED PECANS
2 tablespoons pecans
1 teaspoon extra virgin olive oil
¼ teaspoon sea salt
¼ teaspoon cayenne pepper

VINAIGRETTE
1 tablespoon balsamic vinegar
1 tablespoon extra virgin olive oil
½ onion, chopped (¼ cup)
Sea salt and freshly ground pepper to taste

Make pecans: Preheat oven to 350°F. Combine all ingredients in a small bowl and toss until well coated. Place on parchment-lined baking sheet and bake for 10 minutes, or until toasted, stirring occasionally. Let cool.

Make vinaigrette: Whisk together all ingredients and season with salt and pepper.

Place spinach, pear, and cranberries in a bowl. Add vinaigrette and toss. Transfer to serving bowl and top with pecans. Serve.

Autumn Salad

SALAD

2 tablespoons pumpkin seeds
1 apple, cored and diced
1 tablespoon ground cinnamon
2 cups mixed greens
1 tablespoon dried cranberries
Sea salt and freshly ground pepper to taste

DRESSING

1 tablespoon lemon juice
1 tablespoon red wine vinegar
1 tablespoon extra virgin olive oil
1 garlic clove, minced
½ avocado, peeled, pitted, and diced

Make dressing: Whisk together the juice, vinegar, oil, and garlic. Add avocado.

In a small skillet, toast seeds over low heat for 2 minutes. Remove from skillet and set aside.

In a large bowl, mix apples with cinnamon. Add the baby greens and cranberries. Pour dressing on salad and toss. Transfer to a serving bowl. Top with seeds. Season with salt and pepper. Serve.

White Bean, Beet, and Butternut Squash Salad

serves 1–2

SALAD
1 butternut squash
1 tablespoon extra virgin olive oil
1 teaspoon dried oregano
1 beet, peeled and cubed
1 bunch Swiss chard, chopped (1 cup leaves)
1 15-ounce can cannellini beans, rinsed and drained
1 tablespoon chopped sage

DRESSING
1 tablespoon extra virgin olive oil
1 tablespoon red wine vinegar
Sea salt and freshly ground pepper to taste

Preheat oven to 400°F. Cut squash into thick slices and remove the seeds and skin. Lightly brush the slices on both sides with oil and sprinkle with oregano. Place slices on baking sheet and bake for 15 minutes, turning slices halfway through. Cool completely before cutting into cubes.

Make dressing: In a small bowl, whisk together vinegar and oil. Season with salt and pepper. Set aside.

In a large bowl, combine squash, beets, and beans.

Place chard on serving plate. Add squash, beets and beans. Drizzle dressing over salad and top with sage. Serve.

Nectarine and Watercress Salad

serves 1

SALAD

1 bunch watercress (1 cup leaves)

1 nectarine, halved, stone removed, cut into ½-inch-thick slices

4 cherry tomatoes, halved (¼ cup)

½ cucumber, chopped (¼ cup)

½ onion, chopped (¼ cup)

DRESSING

2 tablespoons balsamic vinegar

1 nectarine, stone removed

2 tablespoons extra virgin olive oil

Sea salt and freshly ground pepper to taste

Make dressing: In a blender or food processor, purée vinegar, nectarine, oil, salt, and pepper until smooth.

Place watercress, nectarine slices, tomatoes, cucumber, and onion in large bowl. Drizzle with dressing and toss. Serve.

Cleansing Fall Salad

serves 1–2

1 cup Brussels sprouts, washed, stems removed

2 carrots, peeled and chopped (¼ cup)

1 apple, cored and diced

2 celery stalks, diced (¼ cup)

2 tablespoons raisins

1 tablespoon lemon juice

Sea salt to taste

1 teaspoon ground cinnamon

Shred Brussels sprouts in a food processor. Transfer to a large mixing bowl. Stir in carrots, apple, celery, and raisins. Add juice and season with salt. Sprinkle with cinnamon. Serve.

Creamy Broccoli Soup

serves 1–2

1 tablespoon coconut oil
1 garlic clove, minced
½ onion, chopped (¼ cup)
½-inch piece fresh gingerroot, peeled and chopped
2 cups broccoli florets
1 bunch spinach (1 cup leaves)
2 cups vegetable broth
1 tablespoon chopped cilantro
½ cup coconut milk
Sea salt and freshly ground pepper to taste

Heat oil in a large pot over medium heat. Stir in garlic, onion, and ginger and sauté for 2 minutes. Add broccoli, spinach, and broth. Bring to a boil. Cover pot and reduce heat to simmer. Cook for about 15 minutes, until broccoli and spinach are tender. Add cilantro and coconut milk. Season with salt and pepper.

Remove pot from stove. Purée the soup in a blender. Serve.

Lentil Stew

serves 1–2

1 tablespoon extra virgin olive oil

½ onion, chopped (¼ cup)

1 garlic clove, minced

½ 15-ounce can diced tomatoes

2 cups vegetable broth

1 celery stalk, chopped

1 carrot, peeled and chopped

¼ teaspoon dried oregano

½ teaspoon cumin

1 cup cooked red lentils (make ahead of time according to package directions)

Sea salt and freshly ground pepper to taste

In a large skillet, heat oil over medium heat and sauté onion for 1 to 2 minutes. Add garlic, tomatoes, broth, celery, carrot, oregano, and cumin and bring to a boil. Reduce heat and simmer for 10 minutes. Place serving of lentils on plate. Top with stew. Season with salt and pepper. Serve.

Kale and Carrot Soup

serves 1–2

4 carrots, peeled, cut into ¼-inch chunks (½ cup)

2 cups vegetable broth

½ 15-ounce can diced tomatoes

1 bunch kale, thinly sliced (1 cup leaves)

1 15-ounce can cannellini beans, rinsed and drained

1 tablespoon balsamic vinegar

1 tablespoon chopped basil

Sea salt and freshly ground pepper to taste

Bring carrots, broth, and tomatoes to a boil in large pot. Add kale, beans, and vinegar. Reduce heat to low and simmer for 7 to 10 minutes. Add basil. Season with salt and pepper. Serve.

Roasted Brussels Sprouts with Mixed Baby Greens Salad

serves 1

1 tablespoon extra virgin olive oil
1 tablespoon apple cider vinegar
1 teaspoon ground nutmeg
1 cup Brussels sprouts, washed, stems removed
1 tablespoon cashews
1 garlic clove, minced
Sea salt and freshly ground pepper to taste
1 bunch mixed baby greens (1 cup leaves)

Preheat oven to 400°F. Coat a baking sheet with the oil.

In a medium bowl, whisk together vinegar and nutmeg. Add in the Brussels sprouts, cashews, garlic, and season with salt and pepper. Stir to coat sprouts. Place on the baking sheet with the cut sides of the sprouts facing down on the pan.

Bake for 20 minutes, flipping sprouts halfway through the baking time.

Place mixed greens on serving plate. Remove Brussels sprouts from baking pan and serve over greens.

Sweater Season Soup

1 tablespoon extra virgin olive oil
½ onion, chopped (¼ cup)
¼-inch piece fresh gingerroot, peeled and chopped
¼ teaspoon ground nutmeg
Sea salt and freshly ground pepper to taste
1 14.5-ounce can pumpkin purée
1 sweet potato, peeled and cut into ¼-inch cubes (2 cups)
2 cups vegetable broth

In a soup pot, heat olive oil over medium heat. Sauté the onion for about 5 minutes, until softened. Stir in the ginger and nutmeg and season with salt and pepper. Simmer for 5 minutes.

Add pumpkin, sweet potato, and broth and stir together. Cover and bring to a slow simmer. Cook for about 15 minutes, until vegetables are tender.

Remove from heat and purée the soup in a blender. Return purée to soup pot. Serve.

Pear, Kale, and Almond Smoothie

Makes approximately 18 ounces

2 cups coconut milk
1 bunch kale (1 cup leaves)
1 pear, cored and quartered
1 tablespoon raw almond butter
1 tablespoon ground flaxseeds

Blend all ingredients and serve.

Start Me Up Smoothie

Makes approximately 18 ounces

2 cups almond milk
1 bunch spinach (1 cup leaves)
1 banana
¼ cup blueberries
1 teaspoon ground allspice
1 tablespoon ground flaxseeds
1 tablespoon pecans

Blend all ingredients except pecans. Top smoothie with pecans and serve.

Red Alert Juice

Makes approximately 12 ounces

2 beets (use the stems)
2 carrots
1 apple, cored and quartered
½ lemon, peeled
¼-inch piece fresh gingerroot

Juice all the ingredients and serve.

CHAPTER 7

Winter Detox Plan

Winter is here. The biting gales of icy wind evoke memories of cracking open a book fireside while the kids play with Legos, spread on their stomachs, enjoying the day off from school. After hours of barreling down frozen hills, conjuring up images of a hot, sweet sip of cocoa with just a hint of whipped cream can bring a smile to anyone's face. Then there's the other side of winter, the ugly, isolating, marrow-eating bluster of awful dark days. Is there a season more wrought with love and hate? I suppose it might depend somewhat on whether you winter by the beach or under a heavy blanket of snow. Either way, there are many lessons taught to us by the coldest winter day, because the extreme conditions cause us to learn about ourselves, to find stillness, to reorient our view of the world. Most of all, we appreciate what we often find ourselves fighting against: balance.

Let me back up for a moment.

During grad school at the University of Pittsburgh, I was leaning against the outside brick wall of the dorm in the early morning, waiting for my friend Michelle to pick me up (we carpooled to class). My wooly scarf scratched at my face and neck. My down coat reached my knees—yeah, even my knees were icing over—and my gloves covered hands that still felt the stab of winter's call through the knit. Standing there, teeth chattering, I looked around and realized I was alone. I strained to hear voices or footsteps crunching over crispy snow. In silence, in the aloneness, sadness washed over me. It was an *aha!* moment of feeling depressed and blue . . . the days were dark, cold, and lonely. A month had gone by with me hunkered down in my dorm room, and it was already the beginning of February; the red and pink hearts hanging in the windows gave the date away.

At the time, I didn't realize that my feelings of sadness were natural. Looking back now, I understand that feeling a bit isolated in winter is normal. In fact, being isolated from time to time can nurture us in ways that it took me a long, long journey to discover. That's because as winter makes demand, balance is struck.

Winter can also enhance community. I remember a time in my mid-twenties where our town came together. While working as a teacher, I also had a part-time job after school as a hostess at a local tavern (they say George Washington ate there), and since that job was so different from working with six-year-olds (well, in some respects, adults were the same!), I looked forward to working my shifts with new friends that were like family.

As any teacher can tell you, there's nothing like an oppressive storm to usher in the unexpected, the lovely, and the gathering of friends when the world shuts down.

It happened during my fourth year of teaching . . . a huge storm hit. Since I owned a Jeep Wrangler (army green with a tan soft-top, I so loved that car!), I got the privilege of shuttling my friends around if they needed to go somewhere. Everything seemed to be closed except my tavern.

Suffering from a good case of cabin fever, my friends and I filtered into the cozy tavern and saddled up to the bar. As we sat, the bar filled with locals, people I hadn't seen in years. As day turned into night, we sat, shooting the shit about nothing, about everything, leading to one of the single most precious days of my life. The easy community, the gathering of friends old and new, with one thing in common: feeling isolated and reaching for connection.

I enjoyed listening to all the tall tales of snow adventures and how each of us was forced by winter to slow down with our lives.

Health Focus: PRESERVING ENERGY AND RESTING

During winter, you need to take extra care of yourself with warmth, reflection and rest. When it comes to nourishment, the foods that take the longest to grow, sweet potatoes, carrots, beets and other root vegetables, will keep you healthy during this time of year. Root vegetables take longer for the body to digest so in turn keep your body warm. They also strengthen the kidneys, which govern the winter season.

The kidneys represent the cycle of transformation: birth, life, and death. The kidneys store energy and are also known as the seat of willpower which generates ambition and time to re-evaluate and reflect. When you are in balance during winter, you have a sparkle in your eye, and are full of vitality and life.

When you are in balance during winter: deep sleep, stillness, warmth, inward, reflect, time to dream, be at home.

If there are imbalances: emotional, frustration, late nights, exhaustion, cold to the bone.

Even in my little apartment, my roommate Cathi and I cooked homemade soups and stews for our friends. We would cuddle up on the couch, sip our wine, and savor the creaminess and warmth of our meal while watching movies, laughing, and telling stories.

Nowadays, sitting by the windowsill in winter and watching the steady, quiet snowfall calms me. As I watch out the window, I enter a meditative state, a soulful connection to my surroundings. I relish the fact that I get to rediscover myself in snow season. I take a look at my New Year's intentions and really hone in on my deeper self. I am "still," which allows me to take a good, hard look at my life.

Expectations are lower during winter. Due to bad weather, no one expects you to make it to every event or social obligation. And the plain fact is that they, too, are going inward and need their own space to rest.

What does all this have to do with food?

We tend to hide behind our food, which means we hide from what is really true to us.

Winter can be the best time to develop a healthy relationship with your food instead of merely passing through meals on the way from one activity to another, shoveling it in mindlessly, or waiting too long too eat until you are starving.

But like any relationship, your interaction with food needs to be attentive, nurturing, and whole.

Take time during the winter season to chew your food, to look at it closely, to smell it and savor it. Turn off the TV. Gather your family around; they've probably become strangers, as my friends had in the hustle and bustle of life. Eat without distractions from your smartphone and be present with your meal. Take a deep breath, say a thank-you, or simply be still over your food before eating. Create the rituals that make food special to building community and connectedness. You'll discover different flavors and textures and possibly cook more at home.

Winter allows you to take a full step back and get closer to yourself.

Winter Menu Plan

SEASONAL WINTER FOODS*

Beets, kale, leeks, parsnips, rutabaga, shallots, sweet potatoes, turnips, winter squash

Apples, pears

*For most who live in temperate climates

	Breakfast	Midmorning Snack	Lunch	Midafternoon Snack	Dinner
DAY 1	Sweet Coconut Quinoa	1 apple with 1 tablespoon raw almond butter	Lentil Salad	celery sticks with Spinach Dip	Mix It Up Veggie Soup
DAY 2	Such a Delight Smoothie	grapes (1 cup)	Get Lucky Beans and Greens	handful raw nuts and seeds (1–2 ounces)	Portobello Bites with Kale
DAY 3	Total Wellness GF Oatmeal	Kick-Start Juice	Mexican Chopped Salad	cucumber and carrot sticks with Hummus**	Winter Veggies and Quinoa
DAY 4	Good Morning Fruit Salad	1 apple with 1 tablespoon raw almond butter	Broccoli and Chickpea Salad	celery sticks with Spinach Dip	Creamy Cauliflower Soup
DAY 5	Power C Smoothie	cucumber and carrot sticks with Hummus	Fancy Spinach Salad	grapes (1 cup)	Spicy Sweet Potato Soup

** Hummus Recipe (see page 79)

	Breakfast	Midmorning Snack	Lunch	Midafternoon Snack	Dinner
DAY 6	Sweet Coconut Quinoa	1 apple with 1 tablespoon raw almond butter	Lentil Salad	celery sticks with Spinach Dip	Mix It Up Veggie Soup
DAY 7	Such a Delight Smoothie	grapes (1 cup)	Get Lucky Beans and Greens	handful raw nuts and seeds (1–2 ounces)	Portobello Bites with Kale
DAY 8	Total Wellness GF Oatmeal	Kick-Start Juice	Mexican Chopped Salad	cucumber and carrot sticks with Hummus**	Winter Veggies and Quinoa
DAY 9	Good Morning Fruit Salad	1 apple with 1 tablespoon raw almond butter	Broccoli and Chickpea Salad	celery sticks with Spinach Dip	Creamy Cauliflower Soup
DAY 10	Power C Smoothie	cucumber and carrot sticks with Hummus	Fancy Spinach Salad	grapes (1 cup)	Spicy Sweet Potato Soup

SHOPPING LIST

Greens

- ☐ 3 bunches spinach
- ☐ 2 bunches kale
- ☐ 1 bunch collard greens
- ☐ 1 head romaine lettuce

Vegetables

- ☐ 1 bag carrots
- ☐ 1 bag celery
- ☐ 4–6 yellow onions
- ☐ 2 butternut squash (or use prepackaged cubes)
- ☐ 2 turnips
- ☐ 4 portobello mushrooms
- ☐ 1 bag frozen broccoli florets
- ☐ 1 bag frozen cauliflower florets
- ☐ 4–6 cucumbers
- ☐ 2 leeks
- ☐ 1 carton cherry tomatoes
- ☐ 3 tomatoes (salad preferred)
- ☐ 4 sweet potatoes

Fresh and Dried Herbs

- ☐ Dried oregano
- ☐ Fresh cilantro
- ☐ Dried thyme

Staples

- ☐ Celtic sea salt
- ☐ Freshly ground pepper
- ☐ Extra virgin olive oil
- ☐ 1 garlic bulb

- ☐ Apple cider vinegar
- ☐ Finely ground flaxseeds

Grains

- ☐ 1 bag gluten-free rolled oats (16 ounces)
- ☐ 1 bag quinoa (14 ounces)

Fruits

- ☐ 2 pears
- ☐ 5–6 apples
- ☐ 2 oranges
- ☐ 1 bunch grapes (green or red)
- ☐ 1 bag frozen mango
- ☐ 3 bananas
- ☐ 3 avocados
- ☐ 1 bag lemons

Shelf Items

- ☐ Raw nuts and seeds (avoid salted, roasted) Suggest 1 bag each: sunflower seeds, pumpkin seeds, chopped walnuts, pine nuts, almonds, and pecans
- ☐ 1 bag green lentils (or 16 ounces from bulk section)
- ☐ 1 8-ounce jar raw almond butter
- ☐ 3 15-ounce cans chickpeas
- ☐ 2 15-ounce cans black beans
- ☐ 2 15-ounce cans black-eyed peas
- ☐ Raisins (unsweetened, natural)
- ☐ Dried cranberries (unsweetened, natural)

Spices

- ❑ Ground cinnamon
- ❑ Ground allspice
- ❑ Turmeric
- ❑ Chili powder
- ❑ Cumin
- ❑ Red pepper flakes
- ❑ Fresh gingerroot

Additional Items

- ❑ 1 32-ounce carton almond milk (unsweetened, original)
- ❑ 2 16-ounce cans coconut milk (unsweetened, light)

- ❑ 1 bottle red wine vinegar
- ❑ 1 bottle balsamic vinegar
- ❑ 4 24-ounce cartons vegetable broth
- ❑ 1 jar tahini (found in nut butter aisle)
- ❑ 1 bottle lemon juice
- ❑ 1 bottle lime juice
- ❑ 1 bottle apple juice (100% juice)
- ❑ 1 bottle Dijon mustard
- ❑ 1 package coconut flakes (unsweetened)

Good Morning Fruit Salad

serves 1

1 banana, chopped
1 apple, sliced
1 tablespoon almonds
1 tablespoon raisins
1 tablespoon coconut flakes
1 teaspoon ground flaxseeds

Mix all ingredients except flaxseeds in a bowl. Sprinkle flaxseeds over salad. Serve.

Total Wellness GF Oatmeal

serves 1

1 cup gluten-free rolled oats
1 cup almond milk
1 tablespoon dried cranberries
1 tablespoon pumpkin seeds
1 tablespoon ground flaxseeds
1 teaspoon ground cinnamon

In a medium-size saucepan, cook oats and milk over medium heat for 5 minutes. Remove from heat and place in bowl. Mix in cranberries, pumpkin seeds, flaxseeds, and cinnamon. Serve.

Sweet Coconut Quinoa

serves 1–2

1 tablespoon chopped walnuts
1 cup cooked quinoa (make ahead of time according to package instructions)
½ banana, chopped
1 tablespoon raisins
1 tablespoon coconut flakes

Place walnuts in a pan over medium heat. Toast for 2 to 3 minutes, until slightly browned. Mix the walnuts with the remaining ingredients in a bowl. Serve.

Get Lucky Beans and Greens

serves 1–2

1 tablespoon extra virgin olive oil

1 15-ounce can black-eyed peas, rinsed and drained

1 tomato, chopped (½ cup)

½ onion, chopped (¼ cup)

1 bunch collard greens, stems removed, cut into ribbons or torn into pieces (1 cup leaves)

1 tablespoon red wine vinegar

1 tablespoon lemon juice

1 tablespoon dried oregano

Sea salt and freshly ground pepper to taste

Heat oil in a medium-size pan over medium-high heat. Add black-eyed peas, tomato, and onion and cook for 2 to 3 minutes. Add collards and cook for 2 minutes. Remove from heat and place mixture in a bowl. Stir in vinegar, juice, and oregano and mix well. Season with salt and pepper. Serve.

Lentil Salad

SALAD

1 cup green lentils, rinsed and drained (make ahead of time according to package directions)

½ onion, chopped (¼ cup)

¼ cup cherry tomatoes, halved

DRESSING

1 tablespoon extra virgin olive oil

1 tablespoon red wine vinegar

1 tablespoon Dijon mustard

1 tablespoon lemon juice

Sea salt and freshly ground pepper to taste

Make dressing: In a bowl, whisk together oil, vinegar, mustard, and juice.

Pour dressing over lentils and add onion and tomatoes. Mix well. Season with salt and pepper. Serve.

Mexican Chopped Salad

serves 1–2

SALAD

½ head romaine lettuce, sliced (1 cup leaves)

½ tomato, chopped (¼ cup)

½ avocado, peeled, pitted, and diced

2 celery stalks, sliced (¼ cup)

1 15-ounce can black beans, rinsed and drained

DRESSING

1 tablespoon extra virgin olive oil

1 garlic clove, minced

½ onion, chopped (¼ cup)

1 tablespoon chopped cilantro

1 teaspoon cumin

1 tablespoon lime juice

Sea salt and freshly ground pepper to taste

Make dressing: Whisk together dressing ingredients in a small bowl.

In a large bowl, toss together lettuce, tomato, avocado, celery, and beans. Add dressing. Season with salt and pepper. Toss again and serve.

Broccoli and Chickpea Salad

serves 1–2

SALAD
1 cup broccoli florets
1 15-ounce can chickpeas, rinsed and drained
½ onion, chopped (¼ cup)
1 tablespoon pine nuts

DRESSING
1 tablespoon extra virgin olive oil
1 tablespoon Dijon mustard
1 tablespoon lemon juice
Sea salt and freshly ground pepper to taste

Steam broccoli florets for 5 minutes, until tender. Place in a bowl and add chickpeas and onion. Toss together and set aside.

Meanwhile, toast pine nuts in a skillet over low heat for 2 to 3 minutes, until they start to pop.

Make dressing: In a small bowl, whisk together mustard, juice, and oil.

Pour dressing over broccoli mixture and top with pine nuts. Season with salt and pepper. Serve.

Fancy Spinach Salad

serves 1

SALAD
1 bunch spinach (1 cup leaves)
½ onion, chopped (¼ cup)
1 apple, cored and thinly sliced
½ cup grapes, halved
1 tablespoon chopped walnuts

DRESSING
1 tablespoon apple cider vinegar
1 tablespoon extra virgin olive oil
Sea salt and freshly ground pepper to taste

Toss salad ingredients in a large bowl.

Make dressing: Whisk together ingredients.

Pour dressing on top of salad and mix well. Serve.

Portobello Bites with Kale

serves 1–2

BITES
2 portobello mushrooms, stemmed and gilled
1 garlic clove, minced
1 teaspoon red pepper flakes
1 bunch kale, chopped (1 cup leaves)

DRESSING
1 tablespoon apple cider vinegar
1 garlic clove, minced
1 tablespoon extra virgin olive oil
Sea salt and freshly ground pepper to taste

Make dressing: In a small bowl, whisk together dressing ingredients.

Preheat oven to 400°F. Arrange mushrooms on a baking dish. Drizzle mushrooms with dressing, cover, and marinate for 10 minutes.

Meanwhile, heat oil in a large pan over medium heat. Add onion and red pepper flakes and cook for 2 to 3 minutes. Add kale and cook for 5 minutes.

Roast mushrooms in oven for 15 minutes. Top with kale mixture and season with salt and pepper. Serve.

Mix It Up Veggie Soup

serves 1–2

1 tablespoon extra virgin olive oil
1 leek (white part only), chopped (1 cup)
1 garlic clove, minced
½ onion, chopped (¼ cup)
1 sweet potato, peeled and cubed (2 cups)
2 carrots, peeled and chopped (¼ cup)
½ cup broccoli florets
2 cups vegetable broth
Sea salt and freshly ground pepper

Heat oil in a large pot over medium heat. Add leek, garlic, and onion and cook for 5 minutes. Add sweet potato, carrot, broccoli, and broth. Bring to a boil. Reduce heat to low and simmer for 20 minutes. Purée soup in a food processor until smooth. Season with salt and pepper. Serve.

Creamy Cauliflower Soup

serves 1–2

2 cups cauliflower florets
½ cup apple juice (unsweetened) or 1 apple, cored and juiced
2 cups vegetable broth
½ onion, chopped (¼ cup)
1 tablespoon cilantro
1 teaspoon turmeric
Sea salt and freshly ground pepper

In a large pan, bring cauliflower, apple juice, broth, onion, and cilantro to a boil over medium heat. Cover and simmer for 15 minutes. Blend mixture in food processor until smooth. Add turmeric and season with salt and pepper. Serve.

Winter Veggies and Quinoa

serves 1–2

1 tablespoon extra virgin olive oil
1 butternut squash, peeled and cubed (1½ cups)
2 carrots, peeled and sliced (¼ cup)
½ onion, sliced (¼ cup)
1 turnip, peeled and chopped (1 cup)
1 tablespoon thyme
1 garlic clove, minced
2 tablespoons balsamic vinegar
½ cup cooked quinoa (make ahead of time according to package directions)
Sea salt and freshly ground pepper to taste

Preheat oven to 400°F. Heat oil in a large pan over medium heat. Add squash, carrots, onion, turnip, and thyme and cook for 5 minutes. Place veggie mixture in a baking pan and roast for 15 minutes.

Meanwhile, add garlic and vinegar to another pan and bring to a boil over medium-high heat. Remove vegetables from oven, then coat with vinegar. Place cooked quinoa on a plate and top with vegetables. Season with salt and pepper. Serve.

Spicy Sweet Potato Soup

serves 1–2

1 tablespoon extra virgin olive oil
½ onion, chopped (¼ cup)
1 garlic clove, minced
1 tablespoon chopped cilantro
½ teaspoon cumin
¾ teaspoon chili powder
¼ teaspoon red pepper flakes
1 sweet potato, peeled and diced (2 cups)
2 cups vegetable broth
Sea salt and freshly ground pepper to taste

Heat oil in a large pot over medium heat. Add onion, garlic, cilantro, cumin, chili powder, and red pepper flakes. Cook for 5 minutes. Add sweet potato and stock and bring to a boil. Lower heat and simmer for 20 minutes. Purée three-quarters of the soup. Pour back into the pot and stir. Season with salt and pepper. Serve.

Such a Delight Smoothie

Makes approximately 18 ounces

2 cups coconut milk
1 bunch kale (1 cup leaves)
½ avocado, peeled and pitted
¼ cup frozen mango
1 tablespoon chopped walnuts
1 tablespoon lime juice

Blend all ingredients and serve.

Power C Smoothie

Makes approximately 18 ounces

2 cups almond milk
1 bunch spinach (1 cup leaves)
1 orange, peeled and quartered
1 tablespoon lemon juice
1 tablespoon ground flaxseeds
½ teaspoon ground allspice

Blend all ingredients and serve.

Kick-Start Juice

Makes approximately 12 ounces

3 celery stalks
1 cucumber
1 pear, stem removed
½ lemon, peeled
¼-inch piece fresh gingerroot

Juice the ingredients and serve.

Spinach Dip

serves 4

1 bunch spinach (1 cup leaves)
1 cucumber, chopped
½ cup water
1 tablespoon lemon juice
1 avocado, peeled and pitted
Sea salt to taste

In a blender or food processor, blend all ingredients until creamy.

Note: If kept in an airtight glass container in the fridge, the dip will last for 4 to 5 days.

CHAPTER 8

"Return to Life" after Detox

NEXT STEPS TO KEEP THE GLOW GOING

Congrats! You are glowing and savoring the *Go Clean, Sexy You* life.

You might be asking yourself, "Now what do I do?" You made so many positive changes for your health that you want to keep it going. It is impossible to be on a detox 24/7, 365 days of the year. You are human, and no one is perfect. In fact, perfection is so boring.

Therefore, as you transition to life after detox, use your own judgment. I personally think that if you try to eat "clean" and live a healthy lifestyle 80 percent of the time, and the other 20 percent you have your glass of wine, coffee, cake . . . you are going to rock it out.

That's why we are here; to rock it out by enjoying life and living healthy for a long time.

Here are the four how-to steps for returning to life after detox:

1. Listen to your body.
2. Make a list of what changes you will implement in daily life. (i.e., what did you like about your detox?).
3. Decide what foods to add back in, slowly, from the eliminated list.
4. Develop your customized "return to life" plan.

Let's look at these steps in more detail.

Step 1: Listen to Your Body

During the detox program, you learned how to connect to your body. What felt good—and what didn't? Listening to your body is important as you transition post-detox. If you want to begin to add in items that were eliminated, do it slowly. You don't want to shock your system. Your body is now pretty clean and might not respond kindly to having that chai latte the morning after. Therefore, take note of how you feel immediately after finishing your detox. This will be encouragement to move slowly and ease into things. You may no longer want what you used to crave before detox. Keep listening to your body. She knows best.

Step 2: Make a List: What Did You Like about Detox?

Did you enjoy the dry brushing? Water with lemon in the mornings? The shot of apple cider vinegar (well, probably not!)? Make a list of five takeaways from the detox that you will incorporate in your new daily routine:

Step 3: Decide What Foods to Slowly Add In

Some foods you may no longer crave. Others you'll want to return to enjoying. Although you do not necessarily have to re-introduce foods in this order, for most this sequence will be the easiest:

- Animal protein (if you eat it)
- Soy
- Dairy
- Gluten
- Caffeine
- Sugar (and processed foods)
- Alcohol (if you drink it)

There are a lot of pros and cons for adding these back into your diet. I highly suggest waiting at least a week to add in alcohol and caffeine. These are highly addictive substances, so be careful. As for sugar and processed foods—there are no benefits to consuming these. Sugar is a drug and very addictive. Not to mention that sugar is linked to chronic diseases such as cancer, diabetes, and heart disease.

Another note related to processed foods: try to eat as whole foods as much as possible. Limit eating foods that come in boxes and have barcodes, as Michael Pollan states in *Food Rules*.

Step 4: Develop Your Own Customized Plan

Remember: Planning = Success.

If you want to continue living the *Go Clean, Sexy You* way, make a plan. It doesn't have to be rigid and strict, but having a guide will ensure your commitment to clean living.

Day 11 (or day 8 if summer/raw) to 1 week after detox,
I will add back into my life: _____

Day 11 (or day 8 if summer/raw) to 1 week after detox,
I will keep these healthy habits: _____

Week 1 to week 2,
I will add back into my life: _____

Week 1 to week 2,
I will keep these healthy habits: _____

Week 2 and beyond,
I will add back into my life: _____

Week 2 and beyond,
I will keep these healthy habits: _____

PARTY IN YOUR PANTRY

Now that you are feeling amazing and "returning to life" after detox, it's time for a pantry make-over. That's right. You have been doing all this good stuff for your body, but many of us revert to old ways if we aren't prepared. It's very hard to resist those cookies and chips in the pantry, so let's talk about some ways to stick to clean eating.

Many times, we have the best intentions to eat healthy, but not having the right goods quickly available and on hand sets us up for failure. How many times have you stared in the fridge, trying to make a decision about what to make for dinner, and then ordered takeout because "there's nothing to eat"?

Making decisions when you are starving isn't the best scenario. Trust me. I've done this countless times, and it never ended well for my tummy or my wallet.

When you are building your pantry, keep this guideline in mind:

> *"If it comes in a box or bag, it's not real food."*
> —Michael Pollan, *Food Rules*

I always think of this quote when I'm out shopping. Sometimes it's hard to not buy something bagged or boxed, but if you stay away from the frozen meals section, you'll be safe. Also, if you are still shopping at supermarkets, keeping away from the center aisles is another good rule.

One more thing, and then I promise we'll get to your pantry party.

Scratch these words off your shopping list FOR GOOD:

- Nonfat
- Sugar-free
- Low-fat
- Whole grain (yep, this is a tricky one!)

Lots of marketing goes into advertising fake food . . . especially that whole grain one. If you look at the package's ingredient list, you'll see that there's a lot of processing going on and that nothing is really "whole."

Okay. Let's start working on your pantry makeover.

First, look at labels, and if you find the following ingredients in your pantry, chuck them. I promise this will help you maintain all that hot goodness from the *Go Clean, Sexy You* detox.

- Hydrogenated fats and partially hydrogenated oils
- Enriched flour (or anything that is "enriched")
- Refined sugars, artificial sweeteners, and high fructose corn syrup (it has lots of names such as *sugar, fructose, sucralose, cane sugar, so be careful)
- Highly processed convenience foods
- Sodas, coffee (any drinks with caffeine and sugar)
- White table salt (replace with sea salt)
- Genetically modified foods (GMO) such as corn, soy, canola, aspartame

Next, go through your spices, herbs, and seasoning mixes. If they are more than a year old, toss them out. Buy certified organic when you replace them. This will guarantee they have not been irradiated during processing.

Finally, choose real food. Real food consists of whole food grown in the ground as well as products with ingredients that you can pronounce (5 or less on the label). I developed the following pantry guide for you. Bring it with you the next time you shop. It lists the best produce, snacks, canned and frozen goods (yep, there are a few I recommend if you need to save time), proteins, oils and more.

As you ease into the clean life, detox, or simply experiment with what works best for your body, use this simple list as a guideline. You won't find foods like mac and cheese or sticks of butter on this list like some others out there . . . because this is a clean, healthy list focusing on plant-based and gluten-free items that feed your soul and allow for more *Go Clean, Sexy You* hotness.

MAKE SURE YOUR CLEAN PANTRY IS STOCKED WITH THESE ITEMS:

Produce

- Greens (kale, collard greens, chard, baby spinach, etc.)
- Carrots
- Cucumbers (for snacks or juices)
- Lemons
- Fresh fruit (apples, bananas for smoothies, pears, etc.)
- Fresh herbs
- Onions
- Garlic

Gluten-Free Grains

- Quinoa (pseudograin)
- Brown rice
- Rolled or steel-cut oats
- Millet

Legumes

- Lentils
- Aduki beans
- Black beans
- Cannellini beans
- Chickpeas
- Split peas

Nuts, Seeds, Dried Fruit

- Nuts (raw; almonds, walnuts, pecans, cashews)
- Seeds (raw; pumpkin, sesame, sunflower)
- Unsweetened dried fruit (raisins, cranberries, dates, etc.)

Raw Butters

- Almond butter
- Cashew butter
- Sunflower butter

Nondairy Milk
- Hemp
- Almond (unsweetened original)
- Coconut (light)
- Flax

Oils, Vinegar, Condiments
- Extra virgin olive oil
- Coconut oil
- Apple cider vinegar
- Dijon mustard
- Tahini
- Balsamic vinegar
- Red wine vinegar

Sweeteners and Spices
- Freshly ground pepper
- Celtic sea salt
- Oregano
- Chili powder
- Ground cinnamon
- Raw honey

Canned Goods
- Beans (black, chickpeas, cannellini)

Frozen Goods
- Veggies (broccoli, peas, etc.)
- Frozen berries (blueberries, strawberries, etc.)

Protein Powder/Supplements
- Ground flaxseeds
- Chia seeds
- Protein powder (hemp, pea, rice—avoid "isolate")

Bonus Recipes

If you need more inspiration for after your *Go Clean, Sexy You* detox, I've got you covered with delicious, seasonal meals. You can even use these during your detox program if you need to switch up a few meals. Go for it!

Note: Most recipes include ingredients you already have from the detoxes but there are a few new ones, such as kalamata olives, so make sure to check your shopping list before you head to the store.

Spring Recipes

Tangy Arugula Salad   *serves 1*

2 clementines, peeled and segmented
1 bunch arugula (1 cup leaves)
¼ cup chopped radishes
½ onion, chopped (¼ cup)
1 tablespoon sesame seeds
1 tablespoon lemon juice
1 tablespoon extra virgin olive oil
Sea salt and freshly ground pepper to taste

Toss all ingredients in a bowl and serve.

Cleansing Beet and Herb Salad

serves 1–2

1 tablespoon almonds
1 tablespoon pumpkin seeds
1 beet, peeled and chopped
1 tablespoon basil, torn
1 tablespoon chopped dill
1 tablespoon chopped cilantro
2 tablespoons lemon juice
1 tablespoon extra virgin olive oil

Preheat oven to 350°F. Place almonds and pumpkin seeds on a baking tray in a single layer. Bake for 3 to 5 minutes. Set aside to cool.

In a large bowl, combine beet and herbs. Add cooled nuts and seeds and stir in juice and oil. Toss and serve.

Spring Green Soup

serves 1–2

2 cups vegetable broth
1 leek (white and light green parts only), sliced (1 cup)
1 cup asparagus, trimmed and cut into 1-inch pieces
1 cup broccoli florets
1 tablespoon chopped chives

In a soup pot, bring broth, leek, asparagus, and broccoli to a boil over medium-high heat. Reduce heat and simmer for 10 minutes, until vegetables are tender. Set aside to cool slightly. Pour into a blender and purée in batches until smooth. Ladle soup into bowls, garnish with chives, and serve.

Green Lentil Soup

1 cup green lentils
2 cups vegetable broth
½ onion, chopped (¼ cup)
1 garlic clove, minced
2 celery stalks, chopped (¼ cup)
1 tablespoon extra virgin olive oil
Sea salt and freshly ground pepper to taste

In a soup pot, bring lentils and broth to a boil. Reduce heat and simmer for 20 minutes.

In a skillet, sauté onion, garlic, and celery in oil over medium heat for 5 minutes. Transfer to a large bowl and add cooked lentils and broth. Season with salt and pepper. Serve.

Raw Eggplant Salad

serves 1–2

---

1 eggplant
2 tablespoons lemon juice
1 tablespoon extra virgin olive oil
Sea salt and freshly ground pepper to taste
2 celery stalks, chopped (¼ cup)
¼ cup kalamata olives, pitted and chopped
1 red bell pepper, seeded and chopped (½ cup)
1 tablespoon chopped basil
Sea salt and freshly ground pepper to taste

Trim ends off eggplant. Cut eggplant lengthwise into quarters, then crosswise into ¼-inch cubes.

In a large bowl, mix juice, oil, and salt and pepper. Add 1 cup of eggplant and stir well. Let sit for 5 minutes. Toss in celery, olives, bell pepper, and basil. Serve.

Watermelon and Tomato Bites   *serves 1–2*

BITES
1½ cups watermelon, seeded and cut into ½-inch cubes
1 tomato, cut into ¼-inch cubes (½ cup)
1 tablespoon sunflower seeds

DRESSING
¼ cup water
1 tablespoon extra virgin olive oil
2 tablespoons chopped mint
2 tablespoons parsley

Make dressing: In a blender or food processor, purée water, oil, mint and parsley until smooth.

Toss tomato and watermelon cubes in a bowl. Drizzle with dressing. Top with seeds and serve.

Spinach Chopped Salad   *serves 1*

1 bunch spinach, chopped (1 cup leaves)
½ head romaine lettuce, sliced (1 cup)
½ onion, chopped (¼ cup)
¼ cup kalamata olives, pitted and chopped
2 tablespoons chopped basil
2 tablespoons lemon juice
1 tablespoon extra virgin olive oil
Sea salt and freshly ground pepper to taste
1 tablespoon chopped pecans

In a large bowl, combine spinach, lettuce, onion, olives, and basil.

In a small bowl, mix juice, oil, and salt and pepper. Pour over salad. Toss and top with pecans. Serve.

Portobello and Guac Treats

2 avocados, peeled, pitted, and mashed
½ onion, chopped (¼ cup)
1 tomato, chopped (½ cup)
1 tablespoon lime juice
1 teaspoon sea salt
2 portobello mushrooms, stemmed and gilled

Make guacamole by combining all ingredients except the mushrooms in a bowl. Scoop the guac into the mushroom caps and serve.

Note: This recipe makes 4 servings of guacamole. Store leftovers in an airtight glass container in the fridge; it will last for 2 to 3 days.

Roasted Brussels Sprouts and Carrots

serves 1–2

½ cup Brussels sprouts, washed and stems removed
1 tablespoon extra virgin olive oil
Sea salt and freshly ground pepper to taste
1 garlic clove, minced
2 carrots, peeled and cut diagonally into ½-inch slices (¼ cup)

Preheat oven to 400°F. Toss Brussels sprouts with oil in a large baking dish and season with salt and pepper. Add garlic and carrots. Bake for 25 minutes, until sprouts and carrots are tender. Serve.

Autumn Soup

serves 1–2

½ 14.5-ounce can sweet potato purée
2 cups vegetable broth
1 bunch spinach, chopped (1 cup leaves)
1 apple, cored and chopped
1 teaspoon ground nutmeg

In a pot over medium heat, cook purée in broth for 15 minutes, stirring occasionally. Add spinach, remove pot from heat, and stir soup until spinach is wilts. Garnish with apple and sprinkle nutmeg on top. Serve.

Spinach, Carrot, and Apple Salad

serves 1–2

1 bunch spinach (1 cup leaves)
2 carrots, peeled and grated (¼ cup)
1 apple, cored and chopped
1 tablespoon apple cider vinegar
1 teaspoon extra virgin olive oil
1 tablespoon lemon juice
1 garlic clove, minced
Sea salt and freshly ground pepper to taste
1 tablespoon raisins (optional)

Arrange spinach on a plate. In a large bowl, combine carrots and apples.

In a small bowl, mix vinegar, oil, juice, and garlic. Stir into carrot mixture, season with salt and pepper, and toss. Scoop over spinach. Top with raisins, if desired.

Red Lentil Bowl

1 cup cooked red lentils (make ahead of time according to package directions)

2 tablespoons chopped walnuts

1 leek (white parts only), chopped (1 cup)

1 tablespoon extra virgin olive oil

1 tablespoon red wine vinegar

¼ cup grapes, halved

1 tablespoon chopped mint

Sea salt and freshly ground pepper to taste

1 cup mixed greens or any dark leafy green (optional)

In a skillet over medium heat, toast walnuts for 2 to 3 minutes, until fragrant. Set aside to cool. In the same pan, sauté leek in oil for 5 minutes. Transfer leek to a large bowl and stir in vinegar. Add cooked lentils, walnuts, grapes, and mint. Season with salt and pepper. Serve over greens, if desired.

Red Pepper Soup with Quinoa   *serves 1–2*

½ onion, chopped (¼ cup)

1 garlic clove, minced

¼ teaspoon red pepper flakes

1 tablespoon extra virgin olive oil

2 red bell peppers, seeded and quartered (2 cups)

2 cups vegetable broth

½ cup cooked quinoa (make ahead of time according to package directions)

1 avocado, peeled, pitted, and cubed

1 tablespoon chopped cilantro

Sea salt and freshly ground pepper to taste

In a saucepan over medium heat, cook onion, garlic, and red pepper flakes in oil for 6 minutes. Add bell peppers and broth and bring to a boil. Reduce heat and simmer for 10 minutes. Set aside to cool slightly. Pour soup into a blender and purée in batches until smooth.

In a small bowl, mix cooked quinoa, avocado, and cilantro. Season with salt and pepper. Ladle soup into bowls and top with a spoonful of quinoa mixture. Serve.

Lucky Soup

serves 1–2

½ onion, chopped (¼ cup)

1 garlic clove, minced

1 tablespoon extra virgin olive oil

2 carrots, peeled and chopped (¼ cup)

1 bunch collard greens, de-stemmed and chopped (1 cup leaves)

1 15-ounce can black-eyed peas, rinsed and drained

½ tablespoon dried oregano

1–2 cups vegetable broth

Sea salt and freshly ground pepper to taste

In a pot over medium heat, sauté onion and garlic in oil for 3 minutes. Add carrots and sauté for 2 minutes. Stir in collard greens, black-eyed peas, oregano, and broth and bring to a boil. Reduce heat, cover, and simmer for 20 to 25 minutes. Season with salt and pepper. Serve.

Winter Vegetable Stew

serves 1–2

½ onion, chopped (¼ cup)

1 tablespoon grated fresh gingerroot

1 tablespoon extra virgin olive oil

1 turnip, peeled and chopped (1 cup)

1 sweet potato, peeled and chopped (1 cup)

2 celery stalks, chopped (¼ cup)

1 teaspoon ground cinnamon

2 cups vegetable broth

In a large pot over medium heat, sauté onion and ginger in oil for 5 minutes. Add turnip, sweet potato, celery, cinnamon, and broth and bring to a boil. Reduce heat, cover, and simmer for 15 minutes. Set aside to cool slightly. Pour soup into a blender and purée in batches until smooth. Serve warm.

Sweet Potato Salad

serves 1–2

1 sweet potato, peeled and cut into ½-inch cubes (1 cup)
1 tablespoon extra virgin olive oil
1 tablespoon lime juice
1 apple, peeled, cored, and sliced
½ onion, chopped (¼ cup)
1 tablespoon chopped cilantro
½ avocado, peeled, pitted, and cubed
2 tablespoons pumpkin seeds

In a pot, cover sweet potato with water and bring to a boil. Cook for 10 minutes. Transfer to a colander and rinse under cold water. Drain well and set aside.

In a large bowl, combine oil, juice, apple, onion, and cilantro. Add avocado and sweet potato. Toss, top with pumpkin seeds, and serve.

Note: Toast pumpkin seeds in a pan for 2 minutes, if you wish.

Desserts

Life would be so sad without dessert, don't you agree?

I put together some of my all-time favorite dessert recipes for you to indulge in after your detox. Make these treats for parties and to wow your friends. They will be surprised to find out that these baked goods don't have flour or added sugars.

Yay Bars

Makes approximately 12 bars

2 cups gluten-free rolled oats
¼ cup hemp protein powder
1 tablespoon pumpkin seeds
1 tablespoon raisins
¼ cup cacao nibs (a little somethin' somethin')
1 cup raw almond butter
¼ cup raw honey

In a large bowl, mix oats, hemp, seeds, raisins, and nibs. In a separate bowl, whisk together nut butter and honey. Pour the mixture into the bowl with dry ingredients. Mix well until everything is sticky. If too dry, add more nut butter.

Press mixture into a shallow 8 x 12-inch baking dish lined with foil or wrap. Cover.

Place in fridge for 3 hours. Cut into bar shapes, wrap, and keep refrigerated until ready to eat.

GF Banana Oat Muffins

Makes 12 muffins

2 cups gluten-free rolled oats
3 ripe bananas, mashed
¼ cup almond milk
2 tablespoons pumpkin seeds
1 tablespoon coconut flakes
2 tablespoons raisins
1 tablespoon ground flaxseeds
1 teaspoon ground cinnamon

Preheat oven to 350°F.

Mix all ingredients in a bowl. Pour mixture into a muffin pan. Bake for 20 to 25 minutes, until slightly brown on top.

Note: I LOVE bananas, and three bananas might be overkill for you, so try two and add more if you wish. You can also use cacao nibs or goji berries instead of my go-to sweet addition, raisins.

Raw Brownie Squares

Makes 6–8 brownies

2 cups cashews (soak overnight)
1 tablespoon walnuts
1 cup raw cacao powder
¼ cup medjool dates, pitted
1 tablespoon coconut oil

In a blender or food processor, blend all ingredients to make a smooth paste.

Line a 8 ¾ x 6-inch baking pan or container with parchment paper. Scrape the mixture into the prepared baking pan and smooth it level with your hands. Refrigerate for 1 hour before cutting into squares.

Minty Chocolate Shake

Makes approximately 18 ounces

2 cups almond milk
1 bunch spinach (1 cup leaves)
½ avocado, peeled and pitted
1 tablespoon mint
2 tablespoons cacao powder

Blend all ingredients and serve.

Chia Rice Pudding

serves 1-2

¼ cup medjool dates
1 cup coconut water
½ teaspoon ground cinnamon
2 tablespoons chia seeds
¼ cup raspberries
1 tablespoon mint

In a blender or food processor, combine dates, coconut water, and cinnamon until smooth. Transfer the mixture to a bowl and add chia seeds. Let the pudding set in the fridge for at least 30 minutes. Garnish with raspberries and mint.

Banana Ice Cream

serves 1

1 frozen banana, peeled
1 frozen clementine, peeled and segmented before freezing
1 teaspoon ground cinnamon

In a blender or food processor, combine all ingredients until soft and creamy. If the consistency is too thick, add 1 tablespoon water while blending. Serve.

Note: Top the ice cream with 2 or 3 sliced strawberries and 1 tablespoon cacao nibs, if you wish.

Power Balls

Makes 35–40 balls

2 cups raw almond butter (you can substitute any raw nut butter)
1 cup raw honey
4 cups gluten-free rolled oats
2 tablespoons coconut flakes OR 2 tablespoons sesame seeds

In a large bowl, mix almond butter and honey together.

In a blender or food processor, blend oats until powdered. Add oats to almond butter mixture. The consistency should be sticky (if too thick, add a little more honey).

With your hands, make 2-inch-wide balls and roll in flakes or seeds. Place balls on wax paper on cookie sheets. Store in fridge for 3 hours before eating.

Note: You can roll the balls in cacao nibs, pumpkin seeds, etc. . . . Go wild! Store balls in freezer for endless access to these protein bites.

Big Love and Thank You

Many thanks for being with me on the *Go Clean, Sexy You* wellness journey. I am forever grateful, and I can't wait to hear about your discoveries throughout the year. We are a part of the growing revolution to not only live a happy, healthy life but also feel sexy while we are at it. As we go about life, doing our thing, drinking our water with lemon, making salad jars, breathing in and out, others are watching us. Soon they, too, will do the same. I love when this happens.

I can't even describe how thankful I am that I get to create my life each day, doing what I love most; teaching, writing, and being with you.

There are many, many people in my life who support me and my soul's work as a health coach and writer. And helped me so much in writing this book.

First I would like to thank the amazing teams at Sparkspress and SheWrites Press; forever thankful for all of you! :

Crystal Patriarche, Brooke Warner, Kristin Bustamante, Kelli Uhrich, Lauren Wise, Tabitha Lahr, Janay Lampkin, and Megan Conner.

And to the following super cool chicks who made me (and the food!) look amazing during the photo shoot: Suni Johnson, Janay Lampkin, Megan Conner, Kristen Ross, Amy Adkins, and Allison Pynn.

My heart is wide open for my amazing friends who stood by me while I create and dream. Some of you have been with me for 30 years! I love each and every one of you.

Kathie Shoop, my dear friend, I don't even know how to thank you. We've been together for over 20 years, and I can't believe you haven't thrown me away! Thank you for always pushing me to strive to be the best version of myself and to share my gifts with the world. You made this book possible.

My family, especially my parents and sister, Tina, for supporting and loving me.

My kiddos, Kate and Jack. You make me laugh and fill my heart with complete joy each and every day. I love you both so much.

So much love to my husband, Kevin. I am overwhelmingly grateful for you. Thank you for always believing in me.

AND a special big love and thanks to all the Clean + Sexy Beasts out there. My clients and readers who are wellness goddesses, doing life the way that makes them feel free, happy and sexy, I appreciate you!

 *Lisa*

Inspiration and Resources

I want you to be armed with all the *Go Clean, Sexy You* information you need!

Free Downloads

I have prezzies for you!

- Return to Life Packet
- Detox Journal
- Shopping lists
- Recipe Cards (for all recipes found in this book, oh yeah!)

You can download these pdfs to use with your *Go Clean, Sexy You* book.

Go here to score you goodies ➜ **www.wholehealthdesigns.com/book**

Support

I'm here to cheer you on as well as support you during your *Go Clean, Sexy You* journey.

Here are some ways I can support you:

- Join the Clean + Sexy Community and cleanse with me during the year. Accountability and love from the group is also included:

www.wholehealthdesigns.com/cleanandsexy

OR pop in on a seasonal cleanse

www.wholehealthdesigns.com/detox

- If you want to eat clean between your seasonal cleanses, I have detailed meal plans you can use. The plans include menus, recipes and shopping lists set up like the cleanses in this book.

http://wholehealthdesigns.com/eat-clean-21

- I post tons of recipes and wellness inspiration on my site so pop over anytime:

www.wholeheatlhdesigns.com

I'm a social kind of girl so if you want to chat, connect with me:

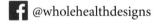 @wholehealthdesigns   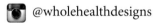 @wholehealthdesigns

 @LisaConsiglioR    @wholehealthdesigns

I want to hear all about the delicious creations you are making in the kitchen!

Also, I LOVE food porn, so tag your photos with **#gocleansexyyou** so I can see what you got cookin' throughout our year together.

Recommended Reading

Staying Healthy with the Seasons
Elson M. Haas, M. D.
*Reference for Seasonal Health
Focus Sections

Food Rules
Michael Pollan

Eat to Live
Joel Fuhrman

The China Study
T. Colin Campbell

Thrive
Brendan Brazier
*Reference for pH balance

Crazy Sexy Diet
Kris Carr

Raw Food Real World
Matthew Kenney and Sarma Melngailis

Integrative Nutrition
Joshua Rosenthal

Heal Your Body
Louise L. Hay

The Alchemist
Paulo Coelho

Clear Your Clutter with Feng Shui
Karen Kingston

The Artist's Way
Julia Cameron

Daring Greatly
Brene Brown, Ph.D.

Breaking Free from Emotional Eating
Ganeen Roth

The Desire Map
Danielle LaPorte

Recommended Kitchen Gear

Besides the Kitchen Gear items I mention in *Go Clean, Sexy You,* I highly recommend investing in the following (these items are *tre'* fun!):

Juicer

There are a lot of juicers to choose from by the best bet is picking a juicer that works with your lifestyle. Also, keep in mind that the price range is wide for juicers, and quality is sometimes the tradeoff. The cheapest ones are often designed poorly and don't yield that much juice from the leafy greens.

Check out these sites for great deals:

Discountjuicers.com
Bestjuicers.com
Amazon.com

Top juicer brands:

Centrifugal: Breville Ikon Multispeed, Omega 4000
Masticating: Champion Juicer
Twin Gear: Green Star Juice Extractor

If you are a newbie, I recommend the Breville Compact Juice Fountain. It's inexpensive (around $99) and quick and easy to use.

Go to my website for the juice product review: **www.wholehealthdesigns.com**

Food Processor

If you have a high-powered blender, you probably wouldn't need a food processor. You can use the Vitamix or Blendec blender for nearly everything. But sometimes you might like a more chunky consistency for your salsas, dips, and dressings, so using a food processor will be the way to go. I recommend Cuisinart but any high-end model should work great.

Dehydrator

Want to make those Kale Chips with a Kick! or try making chips out of sweet potatoes or apples? Even give it a go at making flax crackers or fruit leathers?

I am so forever grateful for my dehydrator! It's a great tool for warming up food instead of using a microwave. Plus you can make delicious snacks!

I recommend the Excalibur. The most practical model is the 9 shelves with 14-inch trays.

Mandolin Slicer

Ahh, the mandolin. This kitchen tool is very inexpensive. It's easy to use, clean and store. Use the mandolin anytime you need things sliced especially when prepping veggies for your week. I make "chippies" at least 5 times a week with my mandolin ("chippies" are my sweet potato chips- yum!). I suggest the Kitchenaid brand.

Spiralizer

This fun gadget is used to make vegetable noodles. Zucchini pasta anyone? I'm pretty obsessed with my Paderno 4-Blade. I use it tons!

Nut Milk Bags

Making your nut milks are healthier and will save you money. So if you want to dip your toe into this type of wellness goodness, I recommend buying nut milk bags. I tried to use cheesecloth and strainers when I first made my milks and it was crazy messy. So purchasing bags, like the P&F All Natural or Ellie's Best will make your smoothies silky smooth. They are inexpensive and can be reused if washed properly.

Coffee Grinder

I know, coffee isn't a part of the *Go Clean, Sexy You* life, but it's a very handy tool for grinding nuts, flaxseeds, and spices. Grab a Hamilton Beach one unless you want a mac daddy Krups. Any type of grinder will work.

Testimonials

I want to share gratitude to all my beautiful Clean + Sexy community, clients and readers. You are beautiful, motivated and inspiring!

Here are their stories:

AMY LUPOZE:

Our lives have changed—permanently. I lost forty pounds, and we ran a 5K for the first time!

I firmly believe that if we had taken a different route, that if we had not found Lisa, (my daughter) Katie would not be where she is today. Lisa's constant support and belief in her made all the difference when everyone else around her didn't believe in her and our chosen method. If we had taken the traditional route of psychologists, etc., I believe Katie would be just like others who struggle with anorexia—in and out of treatment, with no real cure. We have found, through Lisa, not only a solution, but a new way to live our lives. In five short months we achieved what can take others a lifetime. Katie is doing beautifully. She has gained over thirty pounds and is now at a healthy weight. She made honors for the first time in her high school career and was awarded conference honorable mention for softball. We ran a 5K for the first time, and I even lost forty pounds during the program. Our family is continuing on our healthy path. So, while THANK YOU doesn't adequately express our appreciation, the changes Lisa helped us make may very well have saved a life (or two). Thank you, Lisa!

CARRIE SADOWSKI:
I lost ten pounds in six weeks for my cruise!

As a whole, I have a more positive outlook on my health and nutritional needs. I have also allowed myself to take time out of my busy day for some high quality "Carrie" time. It was easy to use the "grab and go" system and not think twice about what I was actually fueling my body with and then providing my body with no rest. Fitness and exercise has always been important to me, but for some reason I never really felt satisfied after a workout and I was so incredibly hungry! After working with Lisa, I now have a better understanding of how to fuel my body and what to fuel it with, so that I can actually feel satisfied throughout the day.

One of my goals was to lose ten pounds in six weeks for this cruise. Lisa taught me how to nourish my body with greens, exercise, sleep, and a more positive inner self-energy. And the ten pounds came off without me even blinking an eye! I feel great and now I am ready for the next ten!

CARRIE HEMMER:
I lost weight, got off my high cholesterol medication, and knocked eleven minutes off my half-marathon race time. Plus my husband's blood pressure is down!

After working with Lisa, I realized how important it is to take time for myself every day and do something that I enjoy or that helps me relax. I do not always think about food—what I am going to eat and when I am going to eat it; measuring the right amount for a serving size. No more of that! I have learned to listen to my body because it will tell me what it needs. I also realized the importance of sleep and how I need good sleep in order to keep moving and stay happy everyday. An occasional nap does wonders! I am more aware of chemicals and toxins that I used to put in my body and on my body. The best hair and skin products are all natural products like coconut oil and dry brushing with rosemary oil.

I have been getting compliments from everyone about how good I look. Everyone wants to know if I have been tanning or on vacation. I have been told that I am glowing—to the point that I thought I might be pregnant!

I have dropped a few pounds, and for the first time in a long time I feel good about my body and appearance. I also have stopped taking my high cholesterol medication. I am faster when I run and go longer distances. I knocked eleven minutes off my race time from last year. I have more energy and feel like I have better focus and memory. My food choices are certainly different. My body now craves healthy food. I try to eat as clean as possible. I have found new loves in juicing and cooking with different grains and veggies/greens.

Lisa has a very positive energy that is contagious to everyone she meets. She has a wonderful passion and love for coaching and counseling people and helping them achieve their goals. Lisa did not try to sway us to conform to healthy eating habits but worked with us in teaching us how to eat what WE liked but in a more healthy, more clean manner.

I think everyone would benefit from nutritional counseling. I thought I was very knowledgeable about health and wellness (little did I know), but now I have a passion for more. I realized all the things I thought I was doing to be healthy and slim down were just working against me. It's not about food, it's about changing your life.

FRANKIE LAMB:
I have tons of energy and completed my first marathon!

As a runner, I knew that nutrition played an important part in the training process, but I did not know HOW to make sure I was properly fueling my body. Well, Lisa changed all that! She taught me what I should be eating pre- and postworkouts. I am eating a greater variety of healthier options such as quinoa, kale, and other greens. I have increased my energy level, and I am cooking more and trying new recipes. Lisa is very positive and motivating. She is so easy to talk to!

BILLIE GARDNER:
When I signed up for Lisa's detox, I was feeling energetically drained. I wanted to feel more vibrant and light.

Some health programs and cookbooks include recipes with unfamiliar and expensive ingredients or the recipes take too much time and energy to create. I wanted to eat healthy, but not spend all day in the kitchen! Lisa's recipes not only are super duper yummy, but they are quick and easy. My hubby loves them too, which is a plus.

I feel amazing when I eat clean and my stomach looks and feels flatter. I'll admit, even though I eat healthy, I slip into bad habits from time to time and Lisa's program gets me back on track and feeling good again! I have a list of recipes for lunch, dinner and snacks that I use over and over that I love.

I'd say the most helpful part of the program is the shopping list. Lisa lists everything I need to purchase at the store that week so all I need to do is go through it and figure out what I already have on hand and what I need to get at the store.

If you're looking to feel light, vibrant, and energized I can't recommend working with Lisa enough!

KRISTIN KING:

I felt energized during my marathon training and was able to easily transition to vegetarianism with Lisa's help.

As a newbie to the world of vegetarianism, I had been searching for a nutritional advisor to assist me in developing a healthy and balanced diet. Also I had an upcoming marathon to train for. The best part about my program with Lisa was that she was very flexible and diverse in her meal plans. She listened to what I liked and tailored her sessions with me. Lisa really focuses on each client individually and what their particular situation is, but her involvement doesn't stop there. Life as a whole is a giant balancing act, and she focuses on all areas of her clients' lives. Throughout my program, I could really see a change in my energy level, and I just felt better overall! When I first started with Lisa, she told me this was going to happen, but I had to feel and see the changes myself to appreciate the work. I am still very surprised at how food affects our bodies and daily life; what goes into our bodies is so vital and now I don't take that for granted anymore. Lisa is a great listener, very in tune to each individual's needs, and as long as you follow her advice, it will help you change your life for the better.

KIMBERLY RIGGINS:

Lisa's done-for-you approach was perfect. All I had to do was buy the ingredients, follow the recipes, and show up.

Moving my body and putting clean food into my mouth are part of my job. In fact, they are the foundation for the work I do with women and their body image issues. However, even I need help once in a while. Working long hours, not getting enough sleep, and overindulging a bit too much, I knew Lisa's program would not disappoint. And I was right!

Lisa's detox program was just the jump start I needed. I wanted to increase my energy, get rid of those pesky sinus issues I was having, and most importantly I didn't want to have to design any of it. It was fantastic. I highly recommend Lisa's detox to anyone who needs a good old-fashioned health boost but doesn't want to forgo real food!

Lisa is inspiring, helpful, and just so darn cute! You will love her programs!

KELLY INNES:

I lost weight, have clearer skin, more energy, a clear mind, and best of all, more patience!

I liked trying all the new foods I was introduced to over the past ten-day detox. Vegetables that I would have passed over in the produce section are now some of my favorites! The ten-day detox is just the beginning. For me it was the beginning of a new outlook on life, on health.

I am transforming the way my entire family eats and lives. This was a great experience, and I can't wait for another cleanse. I've learned so much over these ten days.

CINDY BORCHELT:

Oh, wow, my energy level is great and I lost seven pounds! I feel stronger inside and out! After the first three days, I am sleeping soundly and not having hot flashes! Thank you, Lisa!!!

Lisa's detox is an all-encompassing approach to wellness—yes, foods, but also water, movement, meditation, and—oh, so important—encouragement and support! Also, easy-to-follow shopping list, daily menu, and recipes.

Well, I could go on and on. Lisa is the BEST cheerleader you want on your team! I say that, but her knowledge and gentle approach to every question and concern was such a blessing. I can't wait to detox again!

STEPHANIE ROTH:

I lost four and a half pounds, and I just loved trying all the new recipes! Plus the quality of my sleep was noticeable. I was up before the alarm every day and felt refreshed and ready to face the day ahead.

The recipes were easy to prepare and didn't take much time, which I really appreciated since I work a lot, and it was great knowing I was putting good stuff in my body. Lisa's detox is something you can do for yourself! And it works; you really do feel better. Seeing the improvements made me want more.

BETSY BAUGH:

At the beginning of the ten-day detox, my family was totally against anything to do with it. I was really worried about it—I felt like a lone soldier! By day 2, they were all in—tasting my food, talking it up to their friends, asking questions, etc. It became a family program. I am so excited!

Lisa's pure joy for healthy living is clear and contagious! Lisa's detox left me with confidence, mental clarity, more energy, healthier hair, and a ten-and-a-half-pound weight loss . . . .I know—can you believe it? Thank you, thank you, thank you!

Following this plan is very doable. It's a step-by-step guide to starting a health-focused life. It not only changed my life, it began the process for my entire family.

I thank Lisa for her passion for healthy living, the great recipes, the coaching, and for believing that people can change. Lisa's detox programs are doable. She's now part of the family!

PAM WILLIAMS:

I've been working with Lisa for a few years; I can't believe all that has happened so far. Bottom line, I just feel better. I now look at food from the standpoint of eating for health which has changed my life.

Before I started doing Lisa's programs, I had heard so many different things about eating healthy and doing this or doing that. It was overwhelming actually. I was so busy with work and would grab the most convenient things to eat. I went out to eat a lot. I drank my glass of wine almost every night to relax after a long day. I wasn't sleeping well which resulted in looking tired and feeling tired most of the time. I had puffy eyes and dark circles under my eyes. I also was battling heartburn that I thought was from stress. I was taking sleeping pills at night and drinking caffeine to wake up.

I look at what I used to consider being healthy foods and having to laugh because I was WAY off. I have formed countless healthy habits that I never deviate from. I find myself looking for foods to cure ailments that I have rather than taking meds. My heartburn is gone. I've learned what foods trigger it and needless to say they aren't part of a clean diet. I now sleep better and no longer have that 3 am insomnia, which has been huge for me! Even my husband, Chris, who never in a million years thought he'd like all of this healthy stuff, loves the delicious meals I now cook for us. He even makes us our green smoothies every morning. When I hear him talking to friends or family about our green smoothies it still blows my mind because it is the complete opposite of how we were. I now look at food from the standpoint of eating for health which has changed my life.

NICOLE JEFFERS:
ANYONE can do this detox.

I liked so much about the detox. The recipes were very flavorful, easy to put together, and budget friendly. I liked the support of the community on the blog. Lisa responded very quickly to any comments or questions we had. The education was great, too. Each day there was a new "thing" to try or learn. It was a great experience, and I would definitely do it again!

Lisa gives you all the tools you need, and it is SO good for you! She has tons of knowledge, and the best part is the fact that she cares so much, and it shows.

JEN BARRETT:

The recipes and meal planning were key for me. Plus the shopping list was a real treat. This took so much work and stress out of my life for not having to plan my own meals. I lost weight, gained more energy, have a happier disposition and a renewed energy for life!

I was so pleasantly surprised at how quickly my body turned around. I felt so amazingly good.

I never knew that what I was eating would slow me down so much. I was also pleasantly surprised that my wine cravings decreased. I think the renewed energy allowed me to give up a vice I thought was such a part of me. I am no longer alternating between coffee to wake up and wine to relax. My whole being is just better! I never thought I would be able to go to my favorite Mexican restaurant and NOT drink a delicious margarita or eat chips and cheese dip (a once a week "treat"). It was easy not to eat those things because I just loved the way I felt and didn't want to undo any of what I had worked for. If Lisa told me that in the beginning (and I think she did), I would not have believed her! Amazing! Lisa's detox is doable, delicious, and so worth it. Lisa spreads love and joy wherever she goes, and that's truly refreshing! I loved it!

JENNIFER POLLITE:
It's about so much more than just healthy eating.

Lisa's down-to-earth, accessible program is about more than healthy eating: it's about living a healthy life and taking care of YOU!

She takes you through the whole detoxing process – from prep to detox to easing back into a regular routine. Her suggestions are easy to incorporate, even into the busiest life, and you WILL feel the difference, physically and mentally.

One of my favorite parts is that the recipes are super easy and TASTE REALLY GOOD!!! No starving or eating anything that tastes like cardboard here. That makes it so much easier to keep the healthy life going after the 10 days are over.

Lisa addresses the whole person, and I would recommend her program to anyone looking to improve their health and life.

DR. MARISSA WALLIE:
My cells are singing! I lost five pounds and enjoyed being able to focus on ME!

It is surprising to find out that detox can be easy and really fun. And the food is yummy, too! Lisa's guest experts were such a nice bonus to the program. They really made the detox about body, mind, and spirit.

I praise Lisa for teaching me how to cook healthy, for introducing me to new vibrant foods and recipes, for supporting and loving me, for encouraging me to look inward and focus on ME. I haven't done that in five years (having children changes everything!). I am excited to move forward with life. And to celebrate the big 4-0! Thank you, Coach Lisa!

SHEILA NORMAN:
How to Change Your Life in 10 Short Days!

The first time I heard about a whole foods detox, I thought, "Wow. That's extreme!" Now when people tell me they could never do one, I think, "Wow, are they missing out!"

Lisa's 10-day detox plan is so easy: the hardest part is deciding to do it. She gives you everything you need: from a super-simple menu planner (complete with shopping list and easy-to-follow recipes) to loads of supportive love.

After 10 days, you'll have more energy, clarity, and a strong sense of self and purpose, not to mention glowing skin, radiant hair, and looser clothes! I love the way I felt by Day 6: lighter, clear-headed, full of energy and just really, really good.

The food is really good, and many of the recipes have become staples of my weekly cooking. Best of all, they are all EASY and QUICK! And, it's just real, wholesome food; nothing fancy or weird—just fruits, vegetables, grains, beans and nuts. It's so simple and tasty!

All that said, it's not easy to decide to improve yourself, but I guarantee if you decide to work with Lisa, you'll be glad you did.

LISA KINNEY:
This is not a restriction program. It is a way to become familiar and experiment with whole, fresh, beautiful foods.

Lisa's support was the impetus. I needed to get back on track with my diet, and I feel a whole lot better for it (or, I did, until I had that restaurant meal last night and realize how awful that kind of food makes me feel, even on a short-term basis!). I have more energy (even began to wake up in the morning with positive plans for the day, rather than dragging myself out of bed as had been the case), and more focus, especially for my kids! It's amazing! Also, I have more recipe ideas for breakfast, lunch, dinner, and snacking. Invaluable!

KIM JOHNSON:
As a working mother of two small children, I found myself faced with the challenge of most: I wanted to eat healthier and cleaner but did not have the time or energy to research how to do it.

I am so thankful to have found Lisa. She made the process of integrating "clean, real" food into my diet so easy by providing me with everything I could possibly need to start the process (i.e., recipes, shopping lists, health tips, resources, and tons of ongoing support and encouragement). A big bonus—not only did I enjoy many of the tasty recipes that Lisa provided during the cleanses, but so did my husband and kids! About midway through the first week of my detoxes,

I felt clearer headed and more focused. My husband noticed I was calmer and seemed less stressed. I definitely had increased energy levels, too! There is no reason why Lisa's detox needs to stop completely at the end of two weeks, so I try to incorporate many of the dishes from the cleanse into our regular family meal planning. Suddenly I am abiding by the 80/20 rule without even realizing that I am.

COLLEEN HINDSLEY:
Before working with Lisa, I'd often default to cold cereal for dinner. Now I have a fridge full of ready-to-go options, and I listen to my body so I can make the best choices for ME.

Lisa's recipes are so delicious, like the butternut squash soup, and the pumpkin smoothie was a revelation! I just love that Lisa uses seasonal foods. I've loved learning how to pick fruits and veggies that are in season and getting recipes on how to make delicious meals with them. Aside from the obvious benefits of feeling great due to eating fabulous whole foods, I was less anxious about what to eat and how I would find time to make it. Even though some of my detoxes come at a rough time (I ended up having to travel for work for the better part of two weeks once!), I kept Lisa's advice in mind: listen to my body. It helped keep me sane and also made sure that I made the best choices for me. I've been with Lisa for more than a year and a half, and I must say, she puts together amazing programs and surrounds all the participants with support. Not only do you get a delicious and varied ten-day plan for each season, you also get access to the support and coaching you need to make long lasting changes. Love your programs, Lisa!

DANIELLE FAULKNER:
During Lisa's detox, I lost four and a half pounds and had more energy and focus.

I felt less stressed and healthy from the inside out. I really enjoyed preparing meals again for myself and my family, too. The food was beautiful and so delicious, plus it was a great bonding experience for us.

I was surprised that I could give up caffeine and sugar for ten days.
I love sugar and sweets and I haven't cheated once. It makes such a difference on your overall well-being that giving up something you feel you have to have is just not true. You eat well and will be full. This is a program to jump-start your way to healthy living, and I think everyone can benefit.

I am so thrilled that this was such an eye-opening experience.

I'm an athlete who runs a lot and thought I was taking care of myself. Not! I vow to continue eating greens, vegetables, and fruits. I am a true believer in this and so thankful I joined the ten-day detox!

SUSAN THAXTON:

I found that during the detox, my skin really changed. I lost three pounds, and I broke the sugar cycle, which was the biggest thing for me—no more soda (HUGE goal accomplished—whole reason I did the detox), no more honey in the oatmeal, etc. I was surprised by the fact that I was not crazy tired after the first couple of days!

Lisa's detox program is not seven days of torture and crazy self-denial. It's a chance to find new foods that you may not normally eat, or eat in combination, and find out that they are actually good and do not require a lot of time and effort to make.

I will definitely take many of the recipes with me going forward. They were so easy and tasty. I'm a big fan of the smoothies, and I would never have put kale in a smoothie prior to this. I did the detox to get the sugar out of my life. I have been an avid soda drinker for YEARS—no coffee, just soda. It used to be full-throttle Coke, then Coke Zero. I have been in denial, knowingly so, about needing to end this habit as I justified it by it being my only real vice (I eat pretty well, I'm pretty fit, so why can't I drink soda?). I finally could not deny it any longer and needed to make some changes, and it was a chance to get other sugars out of my diet. I don't eat a lot of "junk" food and don't keep treats in the house, but there was sugar creeping in from other things—honey in the oatmeal, energy bars, etc. This gave me a chance to break the cycle of wanting the sweets. I completely recommend Lisa's program!

SUSAN MCCABE:

I was amazed how good the food was! I loved the meals! I was pleasantly surprised by how easily I was able to stay on track during the detox. Giving up my coffee wasn't as bad as I thought it would be!

I suffered from chronic heartburn that was never "cured" with prescription medication. By the end of the third detox day, I was heartburn-free! I lost weight, and I slept like a baby! Also I loved Lisa's daily blogs and videos where we would hear about her experiences with the detox. A group of us did Lisa's detox together, and we enjoyed e-mailing, texting each other our thoughts on the meals, how we felt, etc. Doing it with the group made it so much fun, and even though I said no to joining Lisa's detox at first (I thought I couldn't give up coffee!), I'm glad I changed my mind. It was an amazing experience!

SUSAN NOBLE:

I went into the detox with quite a bit of skepticism and was convinced I would bail by the middle of the week. After detox, I have never felt better, more energetic, or more clear headed in my life! And I lost five pounds!

Not only did I stick with the program, but I have become a huge cheerleader. It was an amazing experience, and I discovered things about myself that took me by surprise. I never felt deprived. Lisa provides you with complete menus of real food. Nothing too out of the ordinary—well, I don't normally drink smoothies with spinach—but definitely food you find in your grocery store. I will keep most of the recipes and put them in my regular rotation. Looking for a way to kick-start yourself out of the winter rut? This is a great way to do it. (The spinach smoothie sounded awful but it is one of my new favorite things!)

COURTNEY CAHILL:

I lost 7 pounds . . . bye-bye, love handles! And everything was organized for me. Since I'm superbusy, I liked that Lisa's programs are virtual to fit into my schedule.

I've been working with Lisa for a long time, and I've done many detoxes with her and found that my last one has been the "easiest." I attribute it to the healthier habits that I still incorporate from previous detox experiences. I notice things that I never go back to, such as caffeine and gluten. During Lisa's cleanses, I feel good when I wake each morning. I no longer feel weighed down by unhealthy eating habits. My skin, body, and hair all feel different in a very good way. My hair is softer and shinier, and my skin is much clearer and healthier looking. Plus I'm not falling asleep with the TV on! I also love that I'm able to share anything about my experiences without judgment with Lisa and the group. The support makes things so much easier for me!

COURTNEY COBER:

Working with Lisa rocks! I lost weight, got tons of new meal ideas, and I made changes that became second nature, not "diet-y."

My hubby had been diagnosed with high blood pressure and cholesterol before we signed up, and this really helped us get a kick start to correcting those health issues.

During the program, someone at work randomly told me one day how healthy I looked which was the best compliment ever. And ingredients that I would never think to purchase are now staples in our home. Lisa's program is awesome, fun, no pressure and important for healthy living.

DEVON JACKSON:
It was a really fun experience, and I didn't expect that! Plus I started sleeping through the night!

I had increased energy, and I started sleeping through the night for the first time in a long time. It feels magical to wake up and it's actually morning! There's a new awareness of what's good for me and how important it is to take care of myself. Timing is important in order to have the most positive experience, because you might have a really hard time focusing during the first couple of days in a cleanse. It's a great time to do other extra self-care, like the dry brushing, meditation, massage, naps, etc. I LOVED being connected with a community of other cleanse champions. I learned so much from their questions. And hearing the variety of challenges, the optimism and commitment, and Lisa's positive, helpful and wise presence through it all, helped me stay strong and actually made it FUN!

ANGIE FRIDLEY SHELLEM:
I have lost seven pounds total and have been able to keep it off. I feel great and have tons of energy!

My body "fits" again and feels good, and I am keeping the momentum going even after detox. I can't think of a single recipe from the detox that I don't like! The meals are easy to make and very grab-and-go. Since I travel a lot for work, the detox fit into my life perfectly. My face is happy with less breakouts, too! I have found many gluten-free alternatives to the things I love and have been enjoying them in moderation. I think it is the path of the future for me! I've picked up some great habits these last ten days and plan to implement a lot of these recipes in my daily diet. BTW—I absolutely LOVE the lentil bowl. Perfect meal! Thanks for putting together an amazing detox program!

BRIE LANG:
I lost four pounds and I noticed more energy!

I was skeptical at first about the energy, but by day 4, I didn't need the coffee for my 3:30 a.m. departure! Lisa's detox programs are a great reminder of how to eat healthy and control your portions. For a busy mom, the schedule of meals and snacks helped me to stay focused and organized, but with the flexibility to shift around as my schedule or taste buds changed. Trying new recipes with fruits and vegetables helped me to look forward to the meals. Not only were they healthy, but yummy, too. I will continue to use these recipes in my meals and look forward to experimenting with them for new fruits and vegetables.

JENNI ARNOLD:

The menus were easy to follow and the food was delicious! Plus the detox was a good influence on my eight-year-old daughter!

I had more energy, lost several pounds, craved the greens, and loved all the healthy foods! I also loved having the support of the group, and Lisa's e-mails were a big help. I didn't feel "alone" while I was doing the detox. And you still get to EAT during Lisa's detoxes! I loved the whole process!

TRACY SKEELS:

I lost 4 pounds! I'm waking up before the alarm (and I'm awake!). And best of all, Lisa has a variety of easy to prepare recipes with simple ingredients that taste delicious.

I really like the ability to mix up the recipes, make substitutions if I wanted to. I liked the options in the menu supplement to choose from. I love the community check-ins. I appreciate that Lisa takes the time to respond to our posts, questions, and cheer us on. I feel good, no stomachache and no headache. Lisa is incredibly supportive of you during the cleanse. Every email and post is positive and uplifting. I had a fantastic experience!

ANN LASSITER:

Planning is the key, and Lisa has done all the planning for you. Plus doing it with a group makes the detox so much easier.

My group was full of amazingly creative people and amazingly good people to lean on during the detox. I lost weight and wasn't hungry all day. I had better focus because my usual approach to food is to get too busy to eat. So I don't eat for most of the day, then I eat a large meal late. Lisa's menus were helpful, especially that we didn't have to follow them religiously. They allowed some flexibility. AND oh, the recipes were delicious! It wasn't so much that I was glad to see the end of detox, it was more "how can I make parts of this continue to work." I will definitely keep most of the recipes in constant use. Thanks, Lisa!

STEPHANIE KUBICZKI CHRISTNAGEL:

I lost five pounds, I was energized and in a great mood! I felt balanced, and there was no "2:00 p.m." sluggish feeling or sugar crashes.

I felt really great after day 2 and had so much energy even without all the caffeine! I lost five pounds and just feel really healthy! My head was clear and I was more focused. I loved the group support, and had it not been apart of the program I would have failed. Lisa was a great motivator and was also very helpful with any questions I had. All of the recipes were fantastic, too! I'm so glad I participated in Lisa's detox!

CLAIRE MCLELLAN:

I lost seven pounds, slept well and found that I was able to think more clearly. I also noticed a positive effect on my mood and my ability to deal with stressful situations. Plus my husband lost sixteen pounds!

I loved that the menu was all planned out for you in advance and that there was a shopping list as well. It made it so easy to prepare ahead of time. The recipes were simple and delicious. Lisa provided such enthusiastic and positive personal support and a forum for us to receive encouragement from other "detoxers" as well. I looked forward to her video chats and her replies to comments/questions on the blog. I found that it was a great opportunity to assess my eating habits and to try some new foods that I will now add to my repertoire. I also noticed a positive effect on my mood and my ability to deal with stressful situations. The weight loss was a pleasant surprise, and the amount of food (per serving) that we could consume was generous and tasted great!

MELANIE MATTHEWS:

I feel like Lisa's detox programs have been life altering. I've been struggling for the last five years to lose those lingering pounds from two pregnancies. Since my first cleanse with Lisa, I've lost fifteen pounds, and I am almost to my goal weight!

I never felt hungry while doing the cleanses and have taken the recipes and the ingredients to become my staples during the week, while still enjoying my weekends. I thought I was eating healthy before, but this was truly eye-opening. Lisa, thank you for a great program!

JEAN COMPTON:

During the Lisa's detox, I definitely had clearer skin. Glowing skin! And I didn't have that bloated feeling anymore. I loved having Lisa's support with e-mails and check-ins. She throws in bonuses, too!

Something I loved about the detox was committing to the program. I put my mind to it and did it! The recipes were delicious, and I never felt hungry. People should know that the detox is an important thing to do for yourself periodically and on a regular basis. I like the idea of doing it seasonally. You learn new things, check in with yourself—see what's working with your diet, lifestyle, etc., and what isn't. And, it improves the quality of your life!

AMY TOBIAS:

During Lisa's detox, I really did develop the need to eat a lot of greens during the day. My body just felt like it needed the leafy wonders! Plus I noticed clear skin and lost four pounds!

There was so much I loved about my experience. I especially enjoyed the daily, informative affirmations. I loved the fact that Lisa was so positive. I always looked forward to my daily e-mails. Since I feel so good, I want to continue to eat well and keep the glow going!

JULIE HUSSEY:

Lisa's detox made my skin brighter and less puffy. My bloated belly disappeared! I lost four pounds, and I just loved eating healthy and waking up the next day without guilt.

I just FELT GOOD on the detox. Also, I discovered some new foods I didn't know I'd like. Beets! And fennel! I developed some habits, too. The water with lemon in the detox was a supereasy addition to my morning. The recipes were easy to make, and I had many favorites like the hummus, juices, and the salads.

The detox goes by so fast! And you feel so amazing that you don't want to go back to old habits!

MICHAL ALON:

Lisa's detox is just what I needed! I lost 4 pounds, gained TONS of energy, more focus and clarity. AND I'm so much happier!

I was so glad to have someone to take me by the hand and offer huge support as well as super professionalism combined with warm, fun embraces from the group. Lisa's menu plans and recipes are easy to follow and implement as well as fun. It's a celebration . . . self gift days for everyone who wants to improve the quality of their lives in the best supporting and fun environment. I was really impressed with the quality of the programs. And . . . you bet you'll see me in future programs! Detox with Lisa rules!!!!

LISA AULD:

I lost 7 pounds and I feel great. My sugar and carb cravings are gone and I'm enjoying eating all natural foods.

The daily videos from Lisa and guests, the support group, the wide variety of great recipes, the supplemental recipes are what I loved about Lisa's detox. If you are thinking of trying Lisa's detox programs, don't be scared. Her detoxes are different that those crazy ones you hear about. Hers are very doable, and the support from Lisa and fellow detoxers will help you get through your detox with flying colors. After the detox, you will feel great so you will not want to return to previous eating habits. Thanks, Lisa. This is exactly what I needed to get back on track!

MICHELE STANBACK:
My body literally couldn't take my existing diet anymore – after 4 hospital trips in 1 year, I knew Things. MUST. Change.

Before I worked with Lisa, I was bloated, chronically constipated (IBS), and was always in a funk. I knew things had to change, but I needed direction.

Lisa helped me develop sustainable habits that helped me lose 24 pounds of toxic waste, increased my metabolism, and gave me the confidence to pursue my dreams.

Plus, my family benefited! My mother joined me in some of Lisa's fun challenges, and developed cleaner habits that helped her lose 45 pounds and reduce her diabetes medication. She's joining me in the Clean and Sexy community this year—I'm so proud!

KRISTEN MORRISSEY:
My husband told me I have a new glow about me and that he likes my new relaxed, upbeat spirit. Happy surprise! I didn't know detoxing would do this!

Thank you so much for this well organized detox program. It was SUCH a good investment of my time and money. We have 4 kids and over the past 5 years I've been bringing in more and more whole foods and greens and have removed high fructose corn syrup and many processed foods. The kids have mostly responded positively - if its not in the house, they can't eat it (at least here). Our teenager has been the one least interested in "healthy" food, reluctantly eating stuff put in front of him and finding ways to enjoy treats a lot. UNTIL during the detox. I announced at the dinner table that I would be eating a little differently to cleanse my body and feel better. The 13 year old looked up and said "Hey, maybe I'll do that with you." Before I got a chance to pick up my jaw from the floor, our youngest at 7 said "Yeah, maybe I will too." I'm just in shock - happy shock. I'm excited for my family to really FEEL the connection with food and their bodies. Thank you, Lisa!

SUSAN WILLIAMS:
I lost five pounds, and that is hard for me to do, since weight is hard to get off when you are fifty-one years old. I had on a whole just felt better, and I could not get over how good my skin on my face looked. My cravings were fewer, too. My mind was also clear and focused.

Loved this detox! Detox is a good way to keep in touch with your body and inner health. You will lose weight, but it is definitely not like a diet. You are never hungry, whereas on diets you are always hungry. The recipes were awesome, and I can't wait to detox again!

MAGGIE KOLKENA:
Lisa is SINCERELY dedicated to making a positive difference for me. She knows how to work with people from all walks of life—not just people who are already fit and healthy.

I have done detoxes with Lisa, and each time I noticed that I was looking forward to the next meal instead of looking forward to when the whole thing would be over. I've done other plans before, and they are often grimly bland and precious. [Bland = no flavor. Precious = do it exactly this way or it will all be ruined.] But working with Lisa isn't that way. Lisa's recipes are TRULY tasty, and they work for the average person without fancy, odd ingredients. The most luscious result for me was that I slept better after my cleanses and even started drinking delicious green smoothies with her loving support and guidance. Lisa is real and kind.

RACHEL AZALONE:
Since working with Lisa, my mind is clear, I'm sleeping better, and my energy has increased substantially!

Helping people get healthy is my job, but as a busy woman I was finding myself reaching for "healthy" convenience foods instead of truly healthy whole foods. And I was starting to feel the effects! My favorite part of working with Lisa was getting back in touch with real, whole food by focusing on clean eating and preparing meals from scratch. Lisa's program made it super easy. The recipes were simple and delicious—foods that I will continue to eat after the cleanse. During Lisa's detox, I lost five pounds in ten days. Having the meal plan and shopping list laid out for the whole program was really helpful. Lisa's detoxes are perfect to get back on track if you've fallen off the healthy eating wagon and to keep things going after. I lost five pounds during the detox and have been able to maintain healthy habits. I will recommend Lisa to my clients for sure!

NICHOLETTE VON REICHE:
Lisa's detoxes are like your very own Little Black Book of Insider Secrets to looking and feeling AMAZING!

If you want to get your energy, confidence, and health back on track easily and need useful tips and sound advice in a condensed way that fits into your already busy life, Lisa's detox is the "skinny-jean pocket guide" you need at your fingertips. I keep referring to her detoxes when I need to hit the reboot button, but it has also become a weekly resource for meal planning for my family. Lisa's recipes are short, easy to make, super simple to shop for and deliver BIG on taste (my toddler loves it). Even my husband says they are easy to make and taste good (omnivore dude–approved). Lisa has an infectious personality, and I'm so excited to be with her this year and have ongoing support.

ALLYSON TIERNEY:

I loved EVERYTHING about Lisa's program! All of the recipes were delicious, and I really loved that a shopping list was included—really helped me stay organized!

I realized that is was really simple to eat clean; not nearly as daunting as I had imagined. Plus the recipes are amazing…I didn't feel like I was making any sacrifices. AND I had a lot more energy throughout the day. I just adore Lisa and really love how passionate she is about clean eating and her business. Lisa is such a wonderful role model and truly an inspiration.

CAROLINE ARAS:

I have attempted and failed at many strictly "diet" plans. I simply didn't understand until meeting Lisa, that "diet" plans are set up for failure. She taught me, in a very do-able, approachable, manageable program, that integrating heart, mind and body is the dynamic trio to better health, inside and out, regardless of your goal(s): weight loss, improving energy, improved sleep patterns, less aches and pains, etc.

When I first started researching Lisa's program as part of her business, Whole Health Designs, I was immediately struck by three imperatives she embraces:

1. Living a clean and healthy life is not just food and definitely NOT about deprivation. It is about developing awareness for how all parts of our day to day lives affect our well-being, happiness, health and . . . yes, for some of us . . . our weight. This was my first positive "ah ha" moment—approaching my life holistically.

2. Food is love, not the enemy. This was a major paradigm shift in my thinking I still have to work on daily. For decades, food, which I love, was a love/hate relationship every time I opened the refrigerator door. Lisa's program encourages and educates you, without requiring a PhD in nutrition, to make healthy food choices.

3. Partnering & communication are essential to develop and maintain an effective clean

eating lifestyle. Lisa's commitment to her nutritional philosophy, her expertise and desire to be a life-long learner in her field, and her business plan, which is entirely and thoughtfully customer-oriented, have changed my life. As well, her program's on-line accessibility, not only to her but to the entire clean lifestyle community she has created is key.

As with so many of us, my day to day life is so hectic between work and home, that I could feel overwhelmed by any nutrition plan requiring complicated organization and hours in the kitchen prepping food. Lisa's recipes and meal plans are delicious, affordable, realistic and easy.

Index

A

Alcohol, 28, 50, 51, 161

Almond butter

Energy Boost Smoothie, 77

Green Nutty Buddy
Smoothie, 102

Pear, Kale, and Almond
Smoothie, 130

Power Balls, 186

Yay Bars, 181

Almond milk, 34

Chocolate Minty Shake, 184

Cinnamon Roll Millet, 119

Crunch Cereal, 88

DIY Almond Milk, 108

GF Banana Oat Muffins, 182

Green Nutty Buddy
Smoothie, 102

Mango Chia Smoothie, 101

Power C Smoothie, 155

Pumpkin Treat, 119

Start Me Up Smoothie, 130

Strawberry Silk Smoothie, 76

Total Wellness GF
Oatmeal, 144

Almonds

Cleansing Beet and Herb
Salad, 168

Crunch Cereal, 88

DIY Almond Milk, 108

Good Morning Fruit Salad, 142

Peachy Arugula Salad, 90

Animal protein, 19, 23, 28, 161

Apple cider vinegar, 35, 52

Apples

Apple Pie and Banana
Oatmeal, 118

Autumn Salad, 122

Autumn Soup, 176

Cleansing Fall Salad, 125

Crunch Cereal, 88

Fancy Spinach Salad, 150

Good Morning Fruit
Salad, 142

Love Your Liver Juice, 78

Red Alert Juice, 131

Spinach, Carrot and Apple
Salad, 176

Sweet Potato Salad, 180

Warrior Juice, 104

Arugula

Fancy Arugula Salad, 70

Peachy Arugula Salad, 90

Soul-Full Quinoa, 74

Tangy Arugula Salad, 167

Asparagus

Fancy Arugula Salad, 70

Spicy Asparagus Soup, 74

Spring Green Soup, 168

Autumn Salad, 122

Autumn Soup, 176

Avocados

Autumn Salad, 122

Avocado Tomato Salad with
Hot Stuff Dressing, 89

Black Beans and Greens, 70

Chocolate Minty Shake,
184

Creamy Avocado and
Cucumber Soup, 99

Fresh Herb Mango Salad, 92

Guacamole, 98, 172

Light and Cleansing Salad, 91

Mexican Chopped Salad, 148

Portobello and Guac Treats,
172

Pump Up the Iron Salad, 71

Red Pepper Soup with
Quinoa, 178

Silk Berry Smoothie, 102

Spinach Dip, 157

Spring Clean Salad, 67

Strawberry Silk Smoothie, 76

Such a Delight Smoothie, 155

Sweet Potato Salad, 180

Taco Salad, 98

B

Balance, relative, 19, 21

Bamboo cutting boards, 31

Bananas

Apple Pie and Banana
Oatmeal, 118

Banana Ice Cream, 185

Bright and Shiny Smoothie, 76

Energy Boost Smoothie, 77

GF Banana Oat Muffins,
182

Good Morning Fruit
Salad, 142

Green Nutty Buddy
Smoothie, 102

Pineapple Spinach Smoothie, 101
Start Me Up Smoothie, 130
Sweet Coconut Quinoa, 144
Bars, Yay, 181
Beans. *See also* Chickpeas
Black Beans and Greens, 70
canned, 35, 39
cooking, 34, 35, 39
Feeling Light Soup, 75
Get Lucky Beans and Greens, 145
Kale and Carrot Soup, 127
Lucky Soup, 179
Mexican Chopped Salad, 148
soaking, 34
White Bean, Beet, and Butternut Squash Salad, 123
White Bean Dip, 79
Beets
Cleansing Beet and Herb Salad, 168
Red Alert Juice, 131
Tangy Beet Juice, 78
White Bean, Beet, and Butternut Squash Salad, 123
Bell peppers
Avocado Tomato Salad with Hot Stuff Dressing, 89
Chilled Tomato Soup, 94
Peachy Arugula Salad, 90
Ratatouille Supreme, 99
Raw Eggplant Salad, 170
Red Pepper Soup with Quinoa, 178
Spring Renewal Stuffed Peppers, 73
Black Beans and Greens, 70
Blenders, 32–33
Blueberries
Silk Berry Smoothie, 102

Start Me Up Smoothie, 130
Body, listening to, 160
Breathing exercises, 52–53
Bright and Shiny Smoothie, 76
Broccoli
Broccoli and Chickpea Salad, 149
Creamy Broccoli Soup, 126
Lean Up Soup, 72
Mix It Up Veggie Soup, 152
Powerhouse Salad, 91
Spring Green Soup, 168
Brownie Squares, Raw, 184
Brussels sprouts
Cleansing Fall Salad, 125
Roasted Brussels Sprouts and Carrots, 174
Roasted Brussels Sprouts with Mixed Baby Greens Salad, 128

C
Cacao nibs
Yay Bars, 181
Cacao powder
Chocolate Minty Shake, 184
Raw Brownie Squares, 184
Caffeine, 27, 46, 50, 161
Carrots
Cleansing Fall Salad, 125
Kale and Carrot Soup, 127
Lentil Stew, 127
Lucky Soup, 179
Mix It Up Veggie Soup, 152
Red Alert Juice, 131
Roasted Brussels Sprouts and Carrots, 174
Spinach, Carrot and Apple Salad, 176
Tangy Beet Juice, 78
Warrior Juice, 104

Winter Veggies and Quinoa, 153
Cashews
Avocado Tomato Salad with Hot Stuff Dressing, 89
Mushroom Sliders, 96
Raw Brownie Squares, 184
Roasted Brussels Sprouts with Mixed Baby Greens Salad, 128
Spicy Asparagus Soup, 74
Spring Renewal Stuffed Peppers, 73
Cauliflower
Creamy Cauliflower Soup, 152
Powerhouse Salad, 91
Raw Tabbouleh, 100
"Cheesy" Kale Salad, 93
Chia seeds
Chia Rice Pudding, 185
Mango Chia Smoothie, 101
Chickpeas
Broccoli and Chickpea Salad, 149
Chickpea Salad, 68
Fresh Dip, 107
Hummus, 79
Chilled Tomato Soup, 94
Chocolate Minty Shake, 184
Cinnamon Roll Millet, 119
Clean Fifteen, 28, 29
Clean life
definition of, 18
relative balance and, 19
Cleansing Beet and Herb Salad, 168
Cleansing Fall Salad, 125
Clementines
Banana Ice Cream, 185
Tangy Arugula Salad, 167

Coconut

Coconut Berry Quinoa, 64

GF Banana Oat Muffins, 182

Good Morning Fruit Salad, 142

Power Balls, 186

Sweet Coconut Quinoa, 144

Coconut milk, 34

Apple Pie and Banana Oatmeal, 118

Bright and Shiny Smoothie, 76

Chilled Tomato Soup, 94

Creamy Broccoli Soup, 126

DIY Coconut Milk, 108

Energy Boost Smoothie, 77

Lean Up Soup, 72

Pear, Kale, and Almond Smoothie, 130

Pineapple Spinach Smoothie, 101

Silk Berry Smoothie, 102

Such a Delight Smoothie, 155

Coffee grinders, 195

Collard greens

Get Lucky Beans and Greens, 145

Lucky Soup, 179

Constipation, 46

Cosmetics, 55

Cranberries

Autumn Salad, 122

"Cheesy" Kale Salad, 93

Oh So Good Spinach Salad, 120

Total Wellness GF Oatmeal, 144

Creamy Avocado and Cucumber Soup, 99

Creamy Broccoli Soup, 126

Creamy Cauliflower Soup, 152

Crunch Cereal, 88

Cucumbers

Creamy Avocado and Cucumber Soup, 99

Drink Your Veggies Juice, 103

Fresh Dip, 107

Kick-start Juice, 156

Melon Soup, 90

Nectarine and Watercress Salad, 124

Spinach Dip, 157

Warrior Juice, 104

Cutting boards, 31

D

Dairy, 27–28, 50, 51, 161

Dandelion greens

Pump Up the Iron Salad, 71

Dates

Chia Rice Pudding, 185

Raw Brownie Squares, 184

Dehydrators, 195

Desserts

Banana Ice Cream, 185

Chia Rice Pudding, 185

Chocolate Minty Shake, 184

GF Banana Oat Muffins, 182

Power Balls, 186

Raw Brownie Squares, 184

Yay Bars, 181

Detox. *See also individual seasonal plans*

benefits of, 25–26

caloric intake during, 46

common questions about, 44–47

constipation and, 46

daily instructions for, 52–55

drinking water during, 45, 52

exercise and, 45–46, 55

expectations for, 26–27

food allergies and, 46

frequency of, 47

initial symptoms of, 44

journaling about, 54

length of, 42

need for, 24–25

pregnancy and, 42

preparing for, 46, 47, 49–51

returning to life after, 159–62

seasonal foods and, 42

shopping for, 45, 51

special events and, 45

staples, 33–35

substances to skip during, 27–28

substitutions and, 44, 45

supplements during, 54–55

tools for, 30–33, 45

Dips

Fresh Dip, 107

Hummus, 79

Spinach Dip, 157

White Bean Dip, 79

Dirty Dozen, 28–29

DIY Almond Milk, 108

DIY Coconut Milk, 108

Drink Your Veggies Juice, 103

Dry-brushing, 53–54

E

Eggplant

Ratatouille Supreme, 99

Raw Eggplant Salad, 170

80/20 guideline, 18, 159

Energy, storing, 112, 135

Energy Boost Smoothie, 77

Exercise, 45–46, 55

F

Fall detox plan

about, 111–13

health focus of, 112
menu plan for, 114–15
recipes for, 174–77
seasonal foods for, 114
shopping list for, 116–17
Family, support from, 50
Fancy Arugula Salad, 70
Fancy Spinach Salad, 150
Feeling Light Soup, 75
Flaxseeds
Cinnamon Roll Millet, 119
Crunch Cereal, 88
Energy Boost Smoothie, 77
Fresh Dip, 107
GM Gluten-Free Oatmeal, 66
Good Morning Fruit
Salad, 142
Green Nutty Buddy
Smoothie, 102
Pear, Kale, and Almond
Smoothie, 130
Power C Smoothie, 155
Raw Tabbouleh, 100
Silk Berry Smoothie, 102
Start Me Up Smoothie, 130
Total Wellness GF
Oatmeal, 144
Food allergies, 46
Food processors, 195
Fresh Dip, 107
Fresh Herb Mango Salad, 92
Friends, support from, 50
Fruits. *See also individual fruits*
buying, 28–29
Good Morning Fruit Salad,
142

G
Get Lucky Beans and
Greens, 145
GF Banana Oat Muffins, 182

Gluten, 28, 50, 51, 161
GM Gluten-Free Oatmeal, 66
Goals, setting, 50
Good Morning Fruit
Salad, 142
Grains. *See also individual grains*
buying, 39
cooking, 34, 38–39
gluten-free, 33
presoaking, 34
Grapefruit
Light and Cleansing
Salad, 91
Spring Clean Salad, 67
Grapes
Fancy Spinach Salad, 150
Red Lentil Bowl, 177
Green Lentil Soup, 169
Green Nutty Buddy
Smoothie, 102
Greens. *See also individual greens*
Autumn Salad, 122
Black Beans and Greens, 70
Get Lucky Beans and
Greens, 145
Red Lentil Bowl, 177
Roasted Brussels Sprouts
with Mixed Baby Greens
Salad, 128
substituting, 45
Taco Salad, 98
washing, 32
Guacamole, 98, 172

H
Hemp seeds
Crunch Cereal, 88
Pineapple Spinach
Smoothie, 101
Raw Tabbouleh, 100
Herbs, 35, 163

Hummus, 79
Hydration, 83

I
Ice Cream, Banana, 185
Immunity, building, 112
Inflammation, 18
Intention, setting, 50

J
Journaling, 54
Juices
Drink Your Veggies Juice, 103
Kick-start Juice, 156
Love Your Liver Juice, 78
making, 41, 44, 194
Minty Detox Juice, 103
Red Alert Juice, 131
Tangy Beet Juice, 78
Warrior Juice, 104

K
Kale
"Cheesy" Kale Salad, 93
Drink Your Veggies Juice, 103
Kale and Carrot Soup, 127
Kale Chips with a Kick!, 106
Pear, Kale, and Almond
Smoothie, 130
Portobello Bites with Kale, 151
Silk Berry Smoothie, 102
Spring Clean Salad, 67
Strawberry Silk Smoothie, 76
Such a Delight Smoothie, 155
Kick-start Juice, 156
Kidneys, role of, 135
Knives, 30
Kombu, 34

L
Lean Up Soup, 72

Lentils, 34
    Green Lentil Soup, 169
    Lentil Salad, 146
    Lentil Stew, 127
    Pump Up the Iron Salad, 71
    Red Lentil Bowl, 177
    Spring Renewal Stuffed
    Peppers, 73
Lettuce
    Mexican Chopped Salad, 148
    Spinach Chopped Salad, 171
Light and Cleansing Salad, 91
Liver, role of, 58
Love Your Liver Juice, 78
Lucky Soup, 179
Lungs, role of, 112

M
Mandolin slicers, 195
Mangoes
    Black Beans and Greens, 70
    Energy Boost Smoothie, 77
    Fresh Herb Mango Salad, 92
    Mango Chia Smoothie, 101
    Such a Delight Smoothie, 155
Massage, 54
Measuring, 37–38
Melon Soup, 90
Menu plans
    fall, 114–15
    spring, 60–61
    summer, 84–85
    winter, 138–39
Mexican Chopped Salad, 148
Milks, nondairy, 34, 195. *See also* Almond milk; Coconut milk
Millet, 33
    Cinnamon Roll Millet, 119
Minty Detox Juice, 103
Mix It Up Veggie Soup, 152

Muffins, GF Banana Oat, 182
Mushrooms
    Mushroom Sliders, 96
    Portobello and Guac
    Treats, 172
    Portobello Bites with
    Kale, 151
    Soul-Full Quinoa, 74

N
Nectarine and Watercress
    Salad, 124
Nut milk bags, 195
Nuts, 35. *See also individual nuts*

O
Oats, 33
    Apple Pie and Banana
    Oatmeal, 118
    GF Banana Oat Muffins, 182
    GM Gluten-Free Oatmeal, 66
    Power Balls, 186
    Total Wellness GF
    Oatmeal, 144
    Yay Bars, 181
Oh So Good Spinach Salad, 120
Oils, 35
Olives
    Raw Eggplant Salad, 170
    Spinach Chopped Salad, 171
Oranges
    Bright and Shiny
    Smoothie, 76
    Power C Smoothie, 155
    Tangy Beet Juice, 78

P
Pantry, makeover for, 162–65
Parsnips
    Lean Up Soup, 72
    Peachy Arugula Salad, 90

Pears
    Kick-start Juice, 156
    Oh So Good Spinach
    Salad, 120
    Pear, Kale, and Almond
    Smoothie, 130
Peas
    Chickpea Salad, 68
Pecans
    "Cheesy" Kale Salad, 93
    Coconut Berry Quinoa, 64
    Oh So Good Spinach
    Salad, 120
    Pumpkin Treat, 119
    Spinach Chopped Salad, 171
    Start Me Up Smoothie, 130
Pesticides, 28–29
Pesto, 97
pH balance, 19, 21–24
Pineapple Spinach Smoothie, 101
Portobello mushrooms
    Mushroom Sliders, 96
    Portobello and Guac
    Treats, 172
    Portobello Bites with
    Kale, 151
Pots and pans, 31–32
Power Balls, 186
Power C Smoothie, 155
Powerhouse Salad, 91
Precleansing, 49–51
Pregnancy, 42
Processed foods, 27, 46, 50, 161, 163
Pseudograins, 33
Pudding, Chia Rice, 185
Pumpkin
    Pumpkin Treat, 119
    Sweater Season Soup, 129
Pumpkin seeds
    Autumn Salad, 122

Avocado Tomato Salad with Hot Stuff Dressing, 89
Chickpea Salad, 68
Cleansing Beet and Herb Salad, 168
Crunch Cereal, 88
GF Banana Oat Muffins, 182
Pump Up the Iron Salad, 71
Sweet Potato Salad, 180
Total Wellness GF Oatmeal, 144
Yay Bars, 181
Pump Up the Iron Salad, 71

Q

Quinoa, 33
Coconut Berry Quinoa, 64
Pumpkin Treat, 119
Red Pepper Soup with Quinoa, 178
Soul-Full Quinoa, 74
Sweet Coconut Quinoa, 144
Winter Veggies and Quinoa, 153

R

Radishes
Fancy Arugula Salad, 70
Tangy Arugula Salad, 167

Raisins
Cleansing Fall Salad, 125
Crunch Cereal, 88
GF Banana Oat Muffins, 182
GM Gluten-Free Oatmeal, 66
Good Morning Fruit Salad, 142
Powerhouse Salad, 91
Spinach, Carrot and Apple Salad, 176
Spring Renewal Stuffed Peppers, 73

Sweet Coconut Quinoa, 144
Yay Bars, 181

Raspberries
Chia Rice Pudding, 185
Ratatouille Supreme, 99
Raw Brownie Squares, 184
Raw Eggplant Salad, 170
Raw Tabbouleh, 100
Red Alert Juice, 131
Red Lentil Bowl, 177
Red Pepper Soup with Quinoa, 178
Rice cookers, 33
Roasted Brussels Sprouts and Carrots, 174
Roasted Brussels Sprouts with Mixed Baby Greens Salad, 128

S

Salads
Autumn Salad, 122
Avocado Tomato Salad with Hot Stuff Dressing, 89
Black Beans and Greens, 70
Broccoli and Chickpea Salad, 149
"Cheesy" Kale Salad, 93
Chickpea Salad, 68
Cleansing Beet and Herb Salad, 168
Cleansing Fall Salad, 125
Fancy Arugula Salad, 70
Fancy Spinach Salad, 150
Fresh Herb Mango Salad, 92
Good Morning Fruit Salad, 142
in jars, 39–40
Lentil Salad, 146
Light and Cleansing Salad, 91
Mexican Chopped Salad, 148

Nectarine and Watercress Salad, 124
Oh So Good Spinach Salad, 120
Peachy Arugula Salad, 90
Powerhouse Salad, 91
Pump Up the Iron Salad, 71
Raw Eggplant Salad, 170
Raw Tabbouleh, 100
Roasted Brussels Sprouts with Mixed Baby Greens Salad, 128
Spinach, Carrot and Apple Salad, 176
Spinach Chopped Salad, 171
Spring Clean Salad, 67
Sweet Potato Salad, 180
Taco Salad, 98
Tangy Arugula Salad, 167
White Bean, Beet, and Butternut Squash Salad, 123
Salad spinners, 32
Seaweed, 34
Seeds, 35. *See also individual seeds*
Sesame seeds
Power Balls, 186
Tangy Arugula Salad, 167
Shake, Chocolate Minty, 184
Shopping lists
fall, 116–17
spring, 62–63
summer, 86–87
winter, 140–41
Silk Berry Smoothie, 102
Skin
brushing, 53–54
cosmetics for, 55
Small intestine, role of, 83
Smoothies
Bright and Shiny Smoothie, 76

Energy Boost Smoothie, 77
Green Nutty Buddy
  Smoothie, 102
making, 40–41
Mango Chia Smoothie, 101
Pear, Kale, and Almond
  Smoothie, 130
Pineapple Spinach Smoothie, 101
Power C Smoothie, 155
Silk Berry Smoothie, 102
Start Me Up Smoothie, 130
Strawberry Silk Smoothie, 76
Such a Delight Smoothie, 155
Soul-Full Quinoa, 74
Soups
  Autumn Soup, 176
  Chilled Tomato Soup, 94
  Creamy Avocado and
  Cucumber Soup, 99
  Creamy Broccoli Soup, 126
  Creamy Cauliflower
    Soup, 152
  Feeling Light Soup, 75
  Green Lentil Soup, 169
  Kale and Carrot Soup, 127
  Lean Up Soup, 72
  Lucky Soup, 179
  Melon Soup, 90
  Mix It Up Veggie Soup, 152
  Red Pepper Soup with
    Quinoa, 178
  Spicy Asparagus Soup, 74
  Spicy Sweet Potato Soup, 154
  Spring Green Soup, 168
  Sweater Season Soup, 129
Soy, 28, 50, 51, 161
Spices, 35, 163
Spicy Asparagus Soup, 74
Spicy Sweet Potato Soup, 154
Spinach
  Autumn Soup, 176

Avocado Tomato Salad with
  Hot Stuff Dressing, 89
Black Beans and Greens, 70
Chocolate Minty Shake, 184
Creamy Broccoli Soup, 126
Drink Your Veggies Juice, 103
Energy Boost Smoothie, 77
Fancy Spinach Salad, 150
Green Nutty Buddy
  Smoothie, 102
Lean Up Soup, 72
Light and Cleansing Salad, 91
Love Your Liver Juice, 78
Mushroom Sliders, 96
Oh So Good Spinach
  Salad, 120
Pineapple Spinach
Smoothie, 101
Power C Smoothie, 155
Spinach, Carrot and
  Apple Salad, 176
Spinach Chopped Salad, 171
Spinach Dip, 157
Start Me Up Smoothie, 130
Spiralizer, 195
Spring Clean Salad, 67
Spring detox plan
  about, 57–59
  health focus of, 58
  menu plan for, 60–61
  recipes for, 64–79, 167–69
  seasonal foods for, 60
  shopping list for, 62–63
Spring Green Soup, 168
Spring Renewal Stuffed
  Peppers, 73
Squash
  Ratatouille Supreme, 99
  Squash Surprise with Pesto, 97
  White Bean, Beet, and
  Butternut Squash Salad, 123

Winter Veggies and
  Quinoa, 153
Start Me Up Smoothie, 130
Storage containers, 31
Strawberries
  Coconut Berry Quinoa, 64
  Strawberry Silk Smoothie, 76
Stress, effects of, 18
Stretching, 52, 55
Substitutions, 44, 45
Such a Delight Smoothie, 155
Sugar, 27, 46, 50–51, 161
Summer detox plan
  about, 81–83
  health focus of, 83
  menu plan for, 84–85
  recipes for, 88–108, 170–72
  seasonal foods for, 84
  shopping list for, 86–87
Sunflower seeds
  Powerhouse Salad, 91
Supplements, 54–55
Sweater Season Soup, 129
Sweet Coconut Quinoa, 144
Sweet potatoes
  Autumn Soup, 176
  Mix It Up Veggie Soup, 152
  Spicy Sweet Potato Soup, 154
  Sweater Season Soup, 129
  Sweet Potato Salad, 180
  Winter Vegetable Stew, 179
Swiss chard
  Feeling Light Soup, 75
  White Bean, Beet, and
  Butternut Squash Salad, 123

T
Tabbouleh, Raw, 100
Taco Salad, 98
Tangy Arugula Salad, 167
Tangy Beet Juice, 78

Tea, 45
Thankful, 53
Tomatoes
  Avocado Tomato Salad with
    Hot Stuff Dressing, 89
  Chilled Tomato Soup, 94
  Get Lucky Beans and
    Greens, 145
  Guacamole, 98
  Kale and Carrot Soup, 127
  Lentil Salad, 146
  Lentil Stew, 127
  Melon Soup, 90
  Mexican Chopped Salad, 148
  Mushroom Sliders, 96
  Nectarine and Watercress
    Salad, 124
  Portobello and Guac
    Treats, 172
  Ratatouille Supreme, 99
  Taco Salad, 98
  Watermelon and Tomato
    Bites, 171
Tools, 30–33, 45, 194–95
Total Wellness GF Oatmeal, 144
Turnips
  Winter Vegetable Stew, 179
  Winter Veggies and
    Quinoa, 153

V
Vegetables. *See also individual
vegetables*
  buying, 28–29
  Drink Your Veggies Juice, 103
  Mix It Up Veggie Soup, 152
  Winter Vegetable Stew, 179
  Winter Veggies and Quinoa,
    153
Vinegars, 35

W
Walnuts
  Apple Pie and Banana
  Oatmeal, 118
  Crunch Cereal, 88
  Fancy Spinach Salad, 150
  GM Gluten-Free Oatmeal, 66
  Green Nutty Buddy
  Smoothie, 102
  Raw Brownie Squares, 184
  Red Lentil Bowl, 177
  Such a Delight Smoothie, 155
  Sweet Coconut Quinoa, 144
  Taco Salad, 98
Warrior Juice, 104
Water, 45, 52
Watercress Salad, Nectarine
  and, 124

Watermelon
  Melon Soup, 90
  Watermelon and Tomato
    Bites, 171
White Bean, Beet, and
  Butternut Squash Salad, 123
White Bean Dip, 79
Winter detox plan
  about, 133–36
  health focus of, 135
  menu plan for, 138–39
  recipes for, 142–57, 178–80
  seasonal foods for, 138
  shopping list for, 140–41
Winter Vegetable Stew, 179
Winter Veggies and
  Quinoa, 153

Y
Yay Bars, 181
Yeast, nutritional, 35

Z
Zucchini
  Ratatouille Supreme, 99
  Squash Surprise with
    Pesto, 97

ABOUT THE AUTHOR

LISA CONSIGLIO RYAN is a certified Integrative Nutrition Health Coach, and the CEO of Whole Health Designs, LLC, which provides detox programs, plant-based and gluten-free meal plans and private coaching. She has a Bachelor's of Science Degree in Developmental Psychology and a Master's Degree in Education. Lisa has worked with thousands in her Renewal 10 Day Detox programs. Her work has been featured in *Fitness Magazine, Tiny Buddha, Elephant Journal, The Daily Meal* and *Fox News.* She loves green juice, yoga, and hanging out with her husband and two children in Annapolis, Maryland.